Practice Papers for SQA Exams

National 5

Chemistry

Introduction	3
Topic Index	5
Practice Exam A	7
Practice Exam B	33
Practice Exam C	61
Answers	91

© 2014 Leckie & Leckie Ltd
Cover © ink-tank

001/30072014

10 9 8 7 6 5 4 3 2 1

ISBN 9780007504732

Published by
Leckie & Leckie Ltd
An imprint of HarperCollins*Publishers*
Westerhill Road, Bishopbriggs, Glasgow, G64 2QT
T: 0844 576 8126   F: 0844 576 8131
leckieandleckie@harpercollins.co.uk   www.leckieandleckie.co.uk

Publisher: Peter Dennis
Project Manager: Craig Balfour

Special thanks to
Jill Laidlaw (copy edit) and proofread;
Ink Tank (cover design); QBS (layout)

Printed in Italy by Lego, S.P.A.

A CIP Catalogue record for this book is available from the British Library.

Acknowledgements

Images: All images © Shutterstock.com

Illustrations © HarperCollins Publisher

Whilst every effort has been made to trace the copyright holders, in cases where this has been unsuccessful, or if any have inadvertently been overlooked, the Publishers would gladly receive any information enabling them to rectify any error or omission at the first opportunity.

Introduction

The three papers included in this book are designed to provide practice in the National 5 Chemistry course assessment question paper (the examination), which is worth 80% of the final grade for this course.

Together, the three papers give overall and comprehensive coverage of the assessment of **knowledge and its application** as well as the **skills of scientific inquiry** needed to pass National 5 Chemistry. The **Key Area Index** grid on page 5 shows the pattern of coverage of the knowledge in the key areas and the skills across the three papers.

We recommend that candidates download a copy of the course assessment specification from the SQA website. Print pages (8–10) which summarise the knowledge and skills which will be tested.

Design of the papers

Each paper has been carefully assembled to be very similar to a typical National 5 question paper. Each paper has 80 marks and is divided into two sections.

- **Section 1** – objective test, which contains 20 multiple choice items worth 1 mark each, totalling 20 marks.

- **Section 2** – paper 2, which contains restricted and extended response questions worth 1 to 3 marks each, totalling 60 marks.

In each paper, the marks are distributed evenly across all three component units of the course, and the majority of the marks are for the demonstration and application of knowledge. The other marks are for the application of skills of scientific inquiry. We have included open and closed reading questions and have built in opportunities for candidates to suggest adjustments to experimental designs.

Most questions in each paper are set at the standard of Grade C, but there are also more difficult questions set at the standard for Grade A. We have attempted to construct each paper to represent the typical range of demand in a National 5 Chemistry paper.

Using the papers

Each paper can be attempted as a whole, or groups of questions on a particular topic or skill area can be tackled – use the **Key Area Index** grid to find related groups of questions. In the grid, questions may appear twice if they cover more than one skill area. Use the 'Date completed' column to keep a record of your progress.

We recommend working between attempting the questions and studying their expected answers.

You will need a **pen**, a **sharp pencil**, **a clear plastic ruler** and a **calculator** for the best results. A couple of different **coloured highlighters** could also be handy.

Expected answers

The expected answers on pages 91–115 give national standard answers but, occasionally, there may be other acceptable answers. The answers have Top Tips provided alongside each one but don't feel you need to use them all!

The Top Tips include hints on the chemistry itself as well as some memory ideas, a focus on traditionally difficult areas, advice on the wording of answers and notes of commonly made errors.

Grading

The three papers are designed to be equally demanding and to reflect the national standard of a typical SQA paper. Each paper has 80 marks – if you score 40 marks, that's a C pass. You will need about 48 marks for a B pass and about 56 marks for an A. **These figures are a rough guide only.**

Timing

If you are attempting a full paper, limit yourself to **two hours** to complete. Get someone to time you! We recommend no more than 30 minutes for **Section 1** and the remainder of the time for **Section 2**.

If you are tackling blocks of questions, give yourself about a minute and a half per mark, for example, 10 marks of questions should take no longer than 15 minutes.

Good luck!

Topic index

Skill tested	Key area	Practice paper questions S1 = Section 1 S2 = Section 2			Date completed
		Exam A	*Exam B*	*Exam C*	
Unit 1: Chemical changes and structure	Rates of Reaction	**S1:** 1 **S2:** 1b(i)	**S2:** 1b(i), (ii) & (iii)	**S2:** 1a(ii), 1b(i)	
	Atomic structure and bonding related to properties of materials	**S1:** 2, 3, 4, 6 **S2:** 2c(i) (ii), 3	**S1:** 1, 2, 3, 4, 5, 6 **S2:** 2, 3(a)	**S1:** 2, 3, 4, 5, 6 **S2:** 2b(i) & (ii), 3a(i) & (ii), 4b & c	
	Formulae and reaction quantities	**S2:** 2a, 8a(i), 9a	**S2:** 1a, 4b(ii), 9(b), 14c(ii)	**S1:** 8 **S2:** 2a(i), (ii), 4a, 8a,	
	Acids and Bases	**S1:** 12 **S2:** 4a, 5a, b	**S1:** 7 **S2:** 5a(i), 5b, 14c(i)	**S1:** 7 **S2:** 5b, 8c, 14	
Unit 2: Natures chemistry	Homologous series	**S1:** 7, 8, 9 **S2:** 7a(ii), 4c, 6c.	**S1:** 10, 11, 14 **S2:** 6b(i) & (ii), 8a, 8c(ii), 12b	**S1:** 9, 10 **S2:** 6, 9	
	Everyday consumer products	**S1:** 10, 11 **S2:** 7a(i), c(i), 8a(ii) & b, 11, 13c	**S1:** 12, 13 **S2:** 7a, b, c(i), 9a	**S1:** 12, 13 **S2:** 7, 9	
	Energy from Fuels	**S2:** 6(a)	**S2:** 8b	**S1:** 14, 15	
Unit 3: Chemistry in society	Metals	**S1:** 13, 14, 15, 16 **S2:** 12	**S1:** 15, 16, 17 **S2:** 10, 11b	**S1:** 17, 18, 19 **S2:** 8b, 10b & c, 13d, 14	
	Properties of plastics	**S1:** 17 **S2:** 13a & b	**S1:** 18 **S2:** 12a, c & d	**S1:** 16 **S2:** 11	
	Fertilisers	**S1:** 18 **S2:** 9b and c	**S1:** 20 **S2:** 14a, b	**S2:** 13a, b, c and d	
	Nuclear Chemistry	**S1:** 19 **S2:** 10a(i)(ii), b	**S1:** 19 **S2:** 13a & b	**S1:** 20 **S2:** 12	
	Chemical analysis	**S1:** 5, 20	**S2:** 4b(i)	**S1:** 8	

N5 Chemistry Course Skills for	Planning and designing	**S2:** 5(c)	**S1:** 8	**S1:** 1 **S2:** 1b(ii)	
	Selecting and presenting information	**S2:** 1a, 4b	**S1:** 9	**S1:** 11 **S2:** 1a(i), 10a	
	Processing information	**S2:** 1b(i), 2b, 5b 6a, 8a(i), 9c, 10a(ii)	**S2:** 1b(ii), 3b, 4b, 6a(i). 7c(ii), 8b, 9b, 13b	**S2:** 1a(ii), 2a(ii), 11c, 12c, 13d	
	Predicting and generalising	**S2:** 1b(ii), 7b	**S2:** 5a(ii), 6a(ii), 8c(i)	**S2:** 5a(ii)	
	Concluding and explaining	**S2:** 4c, 7c(i), (ii)	**S2:** 1b(i), 8c(ii), 11a,	**S2:** 5a(i),	
	Uncertainties and improvements.	**S2:** 6b	**S2:** 4a		

N5 Chemistry

Practice Papers for SQA Exams

Exam A

Fill in these boxes:

Full name of centre

Town

Forename(s)

Surname

Try to answer all of the questions in the time allowed.

Total marks – 80

Section 1 – 20 marks

Section 2 – 60 marks

Read all questions carefully before attempting.

You have 2 hours to complete this paper.

Write your answers in the spaces provided, including all of your working.

Scotland's leading educational publishers

SECTION 1

1. A gas is given off when zinc reacts with hydrochloric acid.

   An increase in which of the following would result in a slower reaction?

   A   temperature

   B   particle size

   C   concentration of the acid

   D   mass of the zinc

2. Which of the following compounds contains ionic bonds?

   A   Nitrogen hydride

   B   Aluminium chloride

   C   Carbon tetrachloride

   D   Sulfur dioxide

3. A pupil set up the following apparatus.

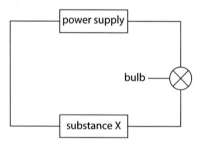

   Which of the following substances would allow the bulb to light?

   You may wish to use your data booklet to help you.

   A   NaCl(s)

   B C_8H_{18}(l)

   C   Hg(l)

   D SiO_2(s)

4. Which electron arrangement is that of an element which is very stable?

    A   2,1

    B   2,8,7

    C   2,8,8

    D   2,2

5. To neutralise 20 cm^3 of a 1 mol l^{-1} solution of sodium hydroxide requires 40 cm^3 of HCl. What is the concentration of the HCl(aq)?

    A   0.1 mol l^{-1}

    B   0.2 mol l^{-1}

    C   0.05 mol l^{-1}

    D   0.5 mol l^{-1}

6. Chlorine has a number of isotopes. Each isotope **must** have

    A   the same atomic number

    B   the same mass number

    C   different electron arrangements

    D   different atomic and mass numbers.

7. What is the name of the following alkane?

    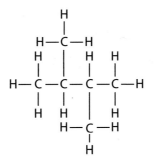

    A   2,3 methylbutane

    B   2,3 dimethylbutane

    C   2,2 dimethylbutane

    D   2,3 dimethylhexane

8. Which of the following reactions can be described as combustion?

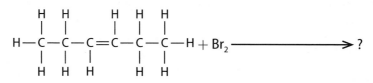

A $\quad 2H_2 + O_2 \longrightarrow 2H_2O$

B $\quad C_2H_4 + H_2 \longrightarrow C_2H_6$

C $\quad C_3H_6 + H_2O \longrightarrow C_3H_7OH$

D $\quad C_8H_{18} \longrightarrow C_3H_6 + C_5H_{12}$

9. Alkenes react with bromine.

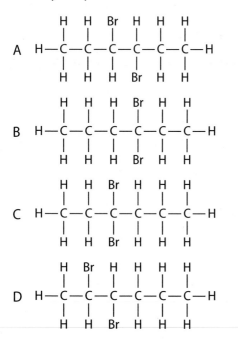

Identify the product of the above reaction.

A, B, C, D

10. Which of the following is a use of esters?

A $\quad$ fuel

B $\quad$ cleaning products

C $\quad$ solvents

D $\quad$ preservatives

11. Which line in the table below matches the family of compounds to its correct functional group?

	Family	Functional group
A	Ester	OH
B	Alcohol	COOH
C	Cycloalkane	OH
D	Carboxylic acid	COOH

12. Which of the following substances reacts with hydrochloric acid to make a gas that turns limewater cloudy?

    A   Magnesium carbonate

    B   Magnesium

    C   Silver oxide

    D   Silver

13. Which of the following metals would result in an increase in voltage if it was used in place of copper in the following cell?

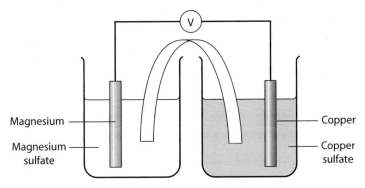

    A   Aluminium

    B   Gold

    C   Iron

    D   Lead

14. Which of the following metals can only be extracted from its ore by electrolysis?

    A   Copper

    B   Lead

    C   Silver

    D   Sodium

15. Iron can be extracted from its ore in a blast furnace.

$$Fe_2O_3(s) + CO(g) \longrightarrow Fe(s) + CO_2(g)$$

Which species is the reducing agent?

A $Fe_2O_3(s)$

B $CO(g)$

C $Fe(s)$

D $CO_2(g)$

16. Which of the following metals would react with zinc bromide?

A Copper

B Lead

C Magnesium

D Tin

17. Which of the following polymers can be described as a condensation polymer?

A Poly(ethene)

B Poly(styrene)

C Poly(ester)

D Poly(propene)

18. The catalyst used in the Haber process is

A Platinum

B Iron

C Copper

D Gold.

19. Different types of radiation have different penetrating properties.

Which type of radiation(s) can be stopped by a thin sheet of aluminium?

A   Alpha only

B   Beta only

C   Alpha and Beta

D   Alpha, Beta and Gamma

20. An unknown solid substance, substance x, was analysed.

1. It neutralises hydrochloric acid, producing a gas.

2. It burns to give off a blue-green colour.

Substance X could be:

You may wish to use your data booklet to help you.

A   Copper

B   Barium oxide

C   Copper carbonate

D   Nickel hydroxide

N5 Chemistry

Practice Papers for SQA Exams

Exam A

Fill in these boxes:

Full name of centre

Town

Forename(s)

Surname

Section 2 – 60 marks

Attempt all questions.

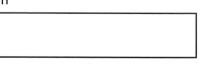

Scotland's leading educational publishers

SECTION 2

1. When magnesium reacts with hydrochloric acid, hydrogen gas is given off.

    The rate of the reaction can be followed by measuring the volume of hydrogen, $H_2(g)$, evolved.

    The table shows the volume of gas given off when excess hydrochloric acid, HCl, is reacted with 0.08 g of magnesium.

Time (s)	Volume of gas (cm³)
0	0
10	14
20	38
40	59
60	69
80	70
100	70

    (a) Plot a line graph of the results of the reaction.   **3**

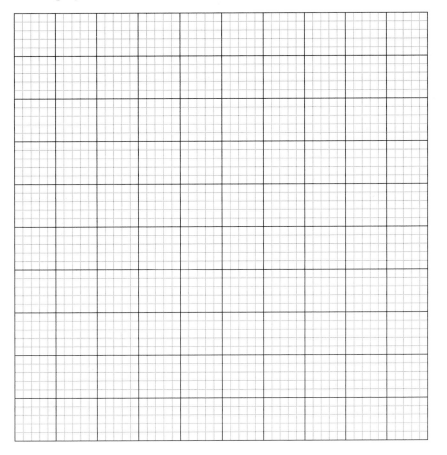

(b) The average rate of the reaction can be measured using data from the graph.

(i) Calculate the rate of the reaction between 10 seconds and 40 seconds. **2**

(ii) The experiment was repeated using 2 mol l^{-1} hydrochloric acid instead of 1 mol l^{-1}.

Predict the average rate of reaction for the same time period as b (i). **1**

Total marks 6

2. Copper is found in the ore Chalcopyrite, $CuFeS_2$.

The iron is removed from the ore to form copper(I)sulfide.

(a) Write the ionic formula for copper(I)sulfide. **1**

(b) When a sample of copper was analysed it was found to be a mixture of two isotopes, ^{63}Cu and ^{65}Cu. The relative atomic mass of copper is 63.5.

Which isotope is the most common? **1**

(c) Copper can form charged particles such as

$$^{63}_{29}Cu^{2+}$$

(i) What name is given to a charged particle like the one above? **1**

(ii) Calculate the number of protons, neutrons and electrons which are in the above charged particle. **2**

Total marks 5

Subatomic particle	Number
Protons	
Neutrons	
Electrons	

3. A pupil analysed a sample of carbon(graphite) and found it to have a high melting point and to conduct electricity as a solid.

The pupil concluded that graphite must have metallic bonding.

Using your knowledge of chemistry, discuss the pupil's conclusion. **3**

Total marks 3

4. Read the passage below and answer the questions which follow.

> ### Ocean acidification
>
> When carbon dioxide (CO_2) is absorbed by sea water, chemical reactions occur that reduce sea water pH, carbonate ion concentration and saturation states of biologically important calcium carbonate minerals. These chemical reactions are termed 'ocean acidification' or 'OA' for short.
>
> Carbon dioxide dissolves in sea water to form carbonic acid (H_2CO_3), which releases some of its hydrogen ions into the sea water. Some of these hydrogen ions then bind to carbonate (CO_3^{2-}) ions in the sea to form bicarbonate ions (HCO_3^-), decreasing the amount of carbonate ions in the water. Since industrialisation (in the 1800s), surface ocean carbonate ion concentrations have declined by 10 per cent in the tropics and southern oceans.
>
> Ocean acidification is expected to impact ocean species to varying degrees. Photosynthetic algae and sea grasses may benefit from higher CO_2 conditions in the ocean, as they require CO_2 to live, just like plants on land. On the other hand, studies have shown that a more acidic environment has a dramatic effect on some calcifying species such as oysters, corals and molluscs.
>
> Calcium carbonate minerals are the building blocks for the skeletons and shells of many marine organisms. In areas where most life now congregates in the ocean, the sea water is supersaturated with respect to calcium carbonate minerals. This means there are abundant building blocks for calcifying organisms to build their skeletons and shells. However, continued ocean acidification is causing many parts of the ocean to become undersaturated with these minerals, which is likely to affect the ability of some organisms to produce and maintain their shell.

This passage was based on an article by the 'Yale Climate Media Forum', http://www.yaleclimatemediaforum. org/2008/06/covering-ocean-acidification-chemistry-and-considerations.

(a) CO_2(g) forms carbonic acid H_2CO_3(aq) when absorbed by sea water.
What evidence is there to show how this acid lowers the pH of the sea?　**1**

(b) Give **one** way in which ocean acidification has benefited some ocean species.　**1**

(c) Since the 1800s the level of industrialisation has grown and therefore the use of alkane based fuels has increased. Explain why this has resulted in an increase in pH levels in the ocean.　**1**

Total marks　3

5. The concentration of hydrochloric acid is often determined by titrating it with a known concentration of sodium carbonate.

The equation for the reaction is:

$$Na^+_2CO^{2-}_3(aq) + 2H^+Cl^-(aq) \longrightarrow CO_2(g) + 2Na^+Cl^-(aq) + H_2O(l)$$

(a) Circle the spectator ions in the above equation.

1

(b) An accurate solution used to determine the concentration of another is often called a standard solution.

(i) Calculate the number of moles of sodium carbonate required to make 250 cm³ of a 0.1 mol l⁻¹ solution.

Show your working clearly.

2

(ii) Using your answer to part (i), calculate the mass of sodium carbonate (Na_2CO_3) needed to make 250 cm³ of a 0.1 mol l⁻¹ solution of sodium carbonate.

Show your working clearly.

2

(c) Two students prepared the standard solution of sodium carbonate using a 250 cm³ volumetric flask.

The notes on the next page were taken from their lab books.

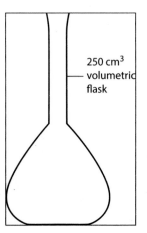

250 cm³ volumetric flask

Student A	Student B
The correct mass of sodium carbonate was weighed out in a beaker.	The correct mass of sodium hydrogen carbonate was weighed out in a beaker.
50 cm^3 of water was added and then stirred with a stirring rod until all the sodium carbonate had dissolved.	50 cm^3 of water was added and then stirred with a stirring rod until all the sodium carbonate had dissolved.
The solution was then transferred to a 250 cm^3 standard flask.	The solution was then transferred to a 250 cm^3 flask.
A further 50 cm^3 of water was added to the beaker, stirred and then added to the standard flask.	A further 50 cm^3 of water was added to the beaker, stirred and then added to the standard flask.
Water was then added up to the 250 cm^3 mark on the standard flask.	150 cm^3 of water was then added to the flask.

Explain which student would have prepared a more accurate solution of sodium carbonate.

2

Total marks 7

6. A pupil carried out an experiment to measure the energy released when pentane (C_5H_{12}) is burned.

The pupil set up the apparatus below.

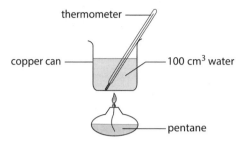

The student recorded the following data:

Mass of pentane	2 g
Volume of water	100 cm^3
Initial temperature of water	21°C
Final temperature of water	29°C
Specific heat capacity of water	4.18 kJkg^{-1}°C^{-1}

(a) Calculate the energy released, in kJ.

   Show your working clearly.   3

(b) Suggest an improvement that could be made to make the experiment more accurate.   1

(c) Pentane belongs to the alkanes.

    (i)   What is the general formula of the alkanes?   1

    (ii)   Draw an isomer of the pentane molecule shown below.   1

Total marks 6

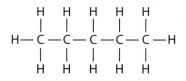

7. The aldehydes are carbon compounds that contain the carbonyl, C=O group at the end of the chain of carbon atoms.

The full structural formula for the first three members is shown below.

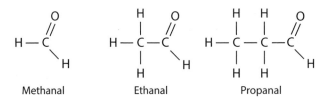

Methanal   Ethanal   Propanal

(a) (i) Draw the full structural formula for butanal.　　　　　　　　　1

(ii) The aldehydes are an example of a homologous series.
What is meant by the term homologous series?　　　　　　　　1

(b) The boiling points of some aldehydes are listed below.

Aldehydes	Boiling point (ºC)
ethanal	20
propanal	49
butanal	76
pentanal	

Predict the boiling point of pentanal, the fifth member of the aldehyde family.　　1

(c) Aldehydes can be made by oxidising alcohols. The reaction is shown below.

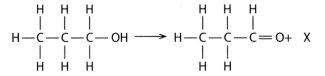

(i) What is element X?　　　　　　　　　　　　　　　　1

(ii) Explain why propan-2-ol cannot be oxidised into an aldehyde.　　　1

Total marks 5

8. (a) Carboxylic acids react with alkalis to produce salt and water.

$$CH_3COOH \quad + \quad NaOH \longrightarrow NaCH_3COO \quad + \quad H_2O$$

Ethanoic acid   Sodium hydroxide   Sodium ethanoate   Water

    (i) What mass of water would be produced if 1.5 g of ethanoic acid was reacted completely with sodium hydroxide?

         Show your working clearly.   **3**

    (ii) Name the salt that would be produced when ethanoic acid reacts with potassium hydroxide.   **1**

(b) Sodium ethanoate and ethanoic acid are mixed to make the flavouring that goes into salt and vinegar crisps.

Give another use for ethanoic acid.   **1**

Total marks 5

9. Ammonia can be produced in the laboratory.

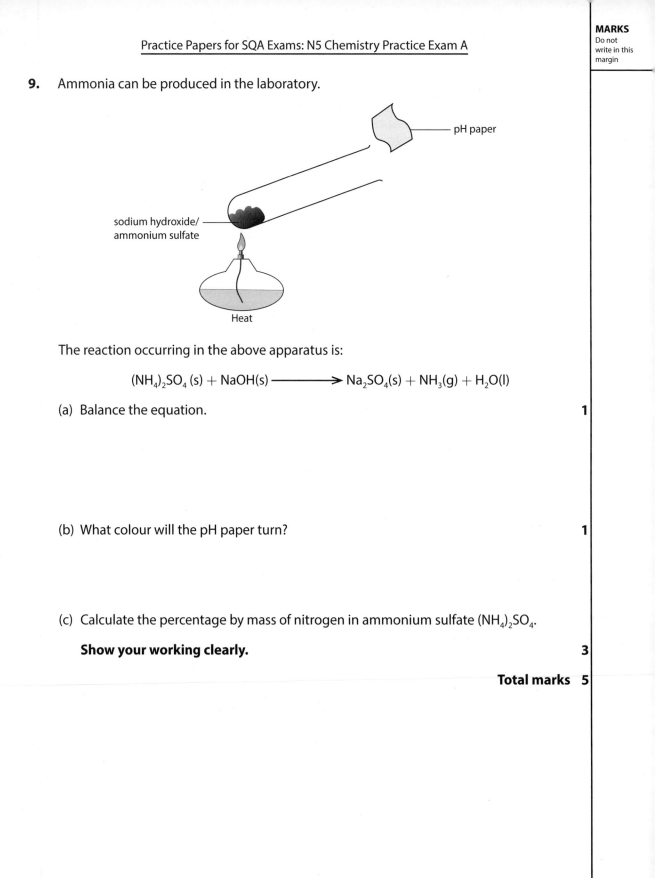

sodium hydroxide/
ammonium sulfate

pH paper

Heat

The reaction occurring in the above apparatus is:

$$(NH_4)_2SO_4 (s) + NaOH(s) \longrightarrow Na_2SO_4(s) + NH_3(g) + H_2O(l)$$

(a) Balance the equation. **1**

(b) What colour will the pH paper turn? **1**

(c) Calculate the percentage by mass of nitrogen in ammonium sulfate $(NH_4)_2SO_4$.

Show your working clearly. **3**

Total marks 5

10. The Voyager 2 satellite has been sending scientific information about our solar system back to Earth for the last 36 years.

Plutonium 238 fuels the satellite.

(a) Plutonium 238 has a half life of 87.7 years.

    (i) State what is meant by the term half life.

1

    (ii) How long would it take for a 20 g sample of Plutonium 238 to decay to 1.25 g?

2

(b) The nuclear equation for the decay of Plutonium 238 is shown below.

$$^{238}_{94}\text{Pu} \longrightarrow\ ^{234}_{92}\text{U} + \text{X}$$

    (i) Name particle X.

1

    (ii) Give **one** reason why Plutonium 238 is a suitable radioactive isotope to fuel the satellite.

1

Total marks 5

11. Oils and fats are found in many foods. Both oils and fats contain fatty acids. The type of fatty acid found in fats and oils are shown below.

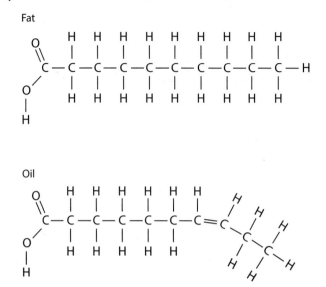

Using your knowledge of chemistry, discuss the differences and/or similarities in the chemical properties of the fatty acids in an oil and fat.　　3

Total marks　3

12. Car manufacturers have developed cars that are powered by hydrogen fuel cells.

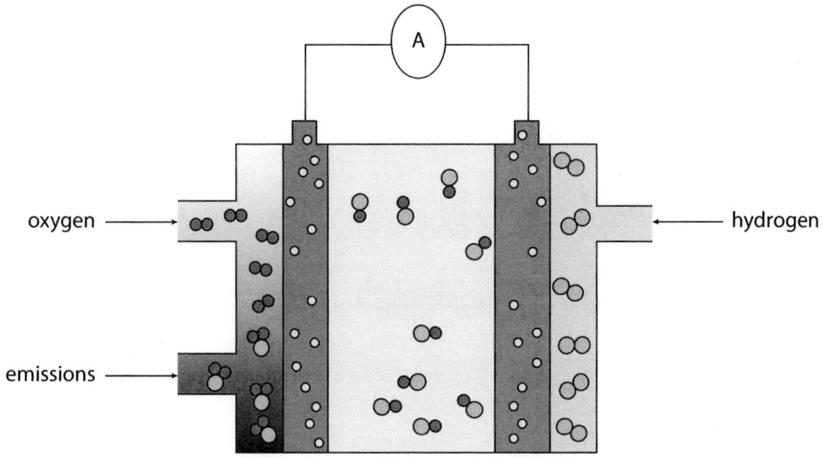

(a) The reaction that takes place at the hydrogen electrode is shown below.

$$H_2(g) \longrightarrow 2H^+(aq) + 2e$$

(i) What name is given to this type of reaction? **1**

(ii) The following reaction takes place at the oxygen electrode.

$$O_2(g) + 4H^+(aq) + 4e \longrightarrow 2H_2O(l)$$

Write the balanced redox equation for the hydrogen fuel cell. **1**

(iii) On the diagram, clearly mark the path and direction of electron flow. **1**

Total marks 3

13. Polymethylmethacrylate (Perspex) is often used as a substitute for glass and is used to make dentures.

The monomer methylmethacrylate is shown below.

(a) Draw a section of the polymer polymethylmethacrylate, showing three monomers joined together.

1

(b) What type of polymerisation takes place to make Perspex?

1

(c) The first contact lenses where hard and made from polymethylmethacrylate. Hydroxyl groups were added to the polymer making it softer and capable of absorbing water.

This development led to soft contact lenses, which we use today.

(i) Circle the hydroxyl group in the monomer hydroxylethylmethacrylate.

1

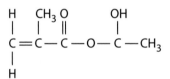

(ii) Apart from the hydroxyl group and C=C, what other functional group is present in the above molecules of hydroxylethylmethacrylate?

1

Total marks 4

Practice Exam B

N5 Chemistry

Practice Papers for SQA Exams

Exam B

Fill in these boxes:

Full name of centre

Town

Forename(s)

Surname

Try to answer all of the questions in the time allowed.

Total marks – 80

Section 1 – 20 marks

Section 2 – 60 marks

Read all questions carefully before attempting.

You have 2 hours to complete this paper.

Write your answers in the spaces provided, including all of your working.

Leckie✕Leckie

Scotland's leading educational publishers

SECTION 1

1. In some countries fluorine is used to reduce tooth decay. Fluorine is an example of

   A   a noble gas

   B   an alkali metal

   C   a halogen

   D   a transition element.

2. What is the symbol for the element which has an ion with the same electron arrangement as neon?

   A   Li

   B   Cl

   C   N

   D   K

3. Which of the following compounds is made up of three elements?

   A   Silicon dioxide

   B   Magnesium nitride

   C   Ammonium hydride

   D   Sodium sulfate

4. Which of the following types of compounds does not conduct electricity as a solid but does as a melt or in solution?

   A   covalent network

   B   ionic

   C   covalent discrete

   D   metallic

5. The shape of an ammonia molecule is shown below.

What name is given to this shape?

A   tetrahedral

B   linear

C   pyramidal

D   bent

6. The bonds which make up a molecule of carbon dioxide (CO_2) can be represented as:

$$O = C = O$$

A molecule of carbon dioxide consists of:

A   two single covalent bonds

B   a single and a triple bond

C   four single covalent bonds

D   two double covalent bonds.

7. Which of the following substances forms an alkali when added to water?
You may wish to use your data booklet to help you.

A   Aluminium oxide

B   Sulfur dioxide

C   Sodium oxide

D   Carbon dioxide

8. The salt copper hydroxide can be prepared by the reacting copper nitrate and sodium hydroxide.

$$Cu(NO_3)_2(aq) + NaOH(aq) \longrightarrow Cu(OH)_2(s) + NaNO_3(aq)$$

Copper hydroxide can be separated from the reaction mixture by

A   evaporating the solution

B   filtering the solution

C   boiling the mixture

D   distilling the mixture.

9. Which of the following hydrocarbons has the highest boiling point?

You may wish to use your data booklet to help you.

A

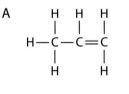

B

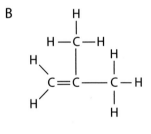

C

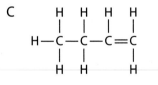

D

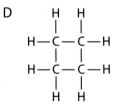

10. Which of the following hydrocarbons is an isomer of 2 methylhexane?

A

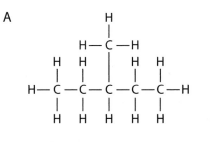

B

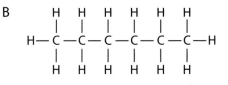

C

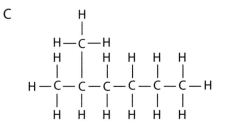

D

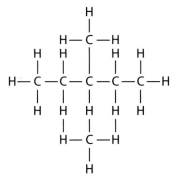

11. The name given to the family of compounds with the general formula C_nH_{2n} is

A   Alkanes

B   Alcohols

C   Cycloalkanes

D   Carboxylic acids.

12. Which of the following is a use of esters?

    A   fuel

    B   cleaning products

    C   solvents

    D   preservatives

13. What is the name of the compound below?

$$CH_3CH_2COOH$$

    A   Ethanol

    B   Ethanoic acid

    C   Propanol

    D   Propanoic acid

14. Which of the following hydrocarbons could be described as saturated?

    A C_2H_2

    B C_2H_4

    C C_2H_6

    D C_3H_6

15. Which of the following metals can be found uncombined in nature?

    A   Aluminium

    B   Copper

    C   Gold

    D   Tin

16. Metal X can be obtained from its oxide by heating with carbon but not by heating alone. Metal X does not react with acids but will react with silver nitrate. Metal X could be:

    A   Iron

    B   Copper

    C   Nickel

    D   Platinum.

17. Iron can be extracted from its oxide by reacting it with carbon monoxide.

$$Fe_2O_3(s) + 3CO(g) \longrightarrow 2Fe(s) + 3CO_2(g)$$

The reducing agent in the above reaction is

A $CO_2(g)$

B $Fe_2O_3(s)$

C $CO(g)$

D $Fe(s)$.

18. Which of the following would be a suitable fertiliser?

You may wish to use your data booklet

A Barium phosphate

B Nickel phosphate

C Ammonium sulphate

D Barium sulphate

19. A radioisotope is used to measure the thickness of paper. Paper is passed under a radioactive source. If the paper is too thick, the intensity of the radiation decreases and the paper is stopped.

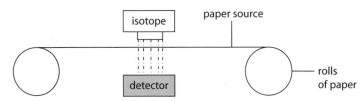

Which isotope would make a suitable source?

Radio isotopes	Half life	Source
A	Long	Alpha
B	Long	Beta
C	Short	Alpha
D	Short	Beta

20. The catalyst used in the production of ammonia is

A   Platinum

B   Aluminium oxide

C   Iron

D   Titanium.

N5 Chemistry

Practice Papers for SQA Exams

Exam B

Fill in these boxes:

Full name of centre

Town

Forename(s)

Surname

Section 2 – 60 marks

Attempt all questions.

Scotland's leading educational publishers

SECTION 2

1.   Aluminium carbonate is one of a number of chemicals used to treat conditions caused by excessive stomach acid, such as heartburn and ulcers. The main acid in stomach acid is hydrochloric acid.

The reaction between aluminium carbonate and hydrochloric acid is shown below.

$$Al_2(CO_3)_3(s) + HCl(aq) \longrightarrow AlCl_3(aq) + H_2O(l) + CO_2(g)$$

(a) Balance the above equation.   1

The speed of the reaction can be followed by measuring the loss in mass.

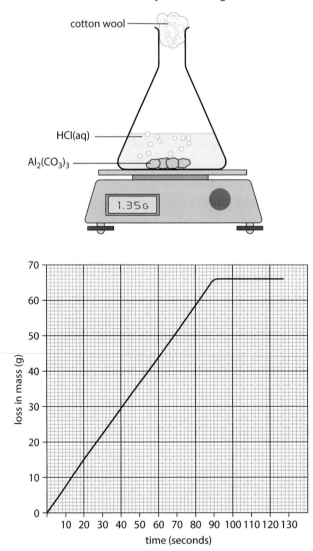

(b) (i) During the reaction the mass of the reacting mixture decreases.

Explain why the loss in mass occurs? **1**

(ii) Using the graph calculate the average rate of reaction, in g s^{-1}, between 20 seconds and 70 seconds. **2**

(iii) The rate of reaction decreases with time.

Explain why the rate of the reaction decreases as the reaction proceeds. **1**

Total marks 5

MARKS
Do not write in this margin

2. (a) Francium, the last natural element, was discovered in 1939.

An ion of this element was found to contain:

87 protons

136 neutrons

86 electrons.

(i) Using the information above, determine the atomic number and mass number.

Atomic number _____

Mass number _____ 1

(ii) Represent this information in the form of a nuclide notation, by filling in the boxes below. 1

 Fr^+

(iii) What is the charge on this ion of Francium? 1

(b) Francium has 33 different isotopes.

What is meant by the word isotope? 1

Total marks 4

3. Read the passage below and answer the following questions.

Oil spillage disasters a thing of the past

Scientists have manufactured a lightweight and reusable material that can absorb up to 33 times its weight in certain chemicals.

'Environmental protection is a globally important issue, especially with so many reports of oil spillage and contaminated rivers due to industry; says study co-author Professor Ian Chen from Deakin University.

Chen and colleagues have developed nanosheets of boron nitride, also called white graphene, which can soak up a wide range of spilled oils, chemical solvents and dyes, such as those discharged by the textile, paper and tannery industries.

Highly porous, the sheets have a high surface area, can float on water, and are water-repellent, the researchers report in the journal *Nature Communications*.

'This material has overall excellent performance compared to other materials;

'One gram of our material will absorb 30 grams of oil', says Chen.

Once the white sheets are dropped on an oil-polluted water surface they immediately absorb the brown oil and become dark brown.

'This process is very fast; after just two minutes, all the oil has been taken up by the nanosheets,' they write.

But rapid absorption isn't the only advantage, Chen says. Once saturated, the sheets can be easily picked up from the water surface and cleaned by burning, heating or washing, to be reused several times.

'Our material can be burned in air to clean all the absorbed oil.

You cannot do this with other carbon-based materials because you burn everything off.'

'After heating the oil-saturated material you can reuse the material again to reabsorb new oil'.

'The ability to recycle makes it a cost-effective alternative', he adds.

This passage was adapted from an article by 'ABC science', Wednesday, 1 May 2013.

(a) Suggest what type of bonding exists in the nanosheet made of boron nitride.

1

(b) How many grams of oil are absorbed by 10 grams of the nanosheet?

1

Total marks 2

4. Tartaric acid is produced when red grapes grow and is the main acid in red wine. Too much tartaric acid will result in the wine being tart and of a poor quality. The concentration of tartaric acid in red wine can be determined by titrating with sodium hydroxide.

$$C_4H_6O_6(aq) + 2NaOH(aq) \longrightarrow Na_2C_4H_4O_6(aq) + 2H_2O(aq)$$

A pupil titrated 25 cm³ of red wine with 0.1 mol l⁻¹ sodium hydroxide. Her results are shown below.

	Titration 1	Titration 2	Titration 3
Volume of NaOH beginning (cm³)	0	12.8	21.7
Volume of NaOH end (cm³)	12.8	21.7	30.4
Total volume of NaOH added (cm³)	12.8	8.9	8.7

(a) Explain why the average volume of sodium hydroxide is taken as 8.8 and not 10.1 cm³.   **1**

(b) (i) Calculate the number of moles of tartaric acid in **25 cm³** of wine.   **3**

(ii) The concentration is recorded as g of tartaric acid per 25 cm³ of wine.

Calculate the mass of tartaric acid in g per 25 cm³ of wine.   **2**

Total marks   6

5. Acids and alkalis can be classed as strong or weak.

Acid	pH	Classification
Nitric	1	Strong
Sulfuric	1	Strong
Carbonic	4	Weak
Ethanoic	4	Weak

Alkali	pH	Classification
Sodium hydroxide	14	Strong
Lithium hydroxide	14	Strong
Ammonium hydroxide	10	Weak

(a) Alkalis neutralise acids to form a variety of salts.

The name and pH of a number of salt solutions are shown below.

Name of salt	pH
Ammonium nitrate	4
Ammonium carbonate	7
Sodium sulfate	7
Sodium carbonate	9

(i) State the classification of acid and alkali that react together to form an acidic salt.

1

(ii) Predict the pH of the salt produced when lithium hydroxide reacts with sulfuric acid.

1

(b) A student investigated how the pH of an acid could be increased to 7, a neutral solution. Using your knowledge of chemistry, discuss how the pH of an acid could be increased to form a neutral solution by substances other than alkalis.

3

Total marks 5

6. The alkynes are a group of compounds that contain a carbon to carbon triple bond.

$H-C\equiv C-H$	ethyne
$H-C\equiv C-\overset{\overset{\displaystyle H}{\mid}}{\underset{\underset{\displaystyle H}{\mid}}{C}}-H$	propyne
$H-C\equiv C-\overset{\overset{\displaystyle H}{\mid}}{\underset{\underset{\displaystyle H}{\mid}}{C}}-\overset{\overset{\displaystyle H}{\mid}}{\underset{\underset{\displaystyle H}{\mid}}{C}}-H$	but-1-yne
$H-\overset{\overset{\displaystyle H}{\mid}}{\underset{\underset{\displaystyle H}{\mid}}{C}}-C\equiv C-\overset{\overset{\displaystyle H}{\mid}}{\underset{\underset{\displaystyle H}{\mid}}{C}}-H$	but-2-yne
$H-C\equiv C-\overset{\overset{\displaystyle H}{\mid}}{\underset{\underset{\displaystyle H}{\mid}}{C}}-\overset{\overset{\displaystyle H}{\mid}}{\underset{\underset{\displaystyle H}{\mid}}{C}}-\overset{\overset{\displaystyle H}{\mid}}{\underset{\underset{\displaystyle H}{\mid}}{C}}-H$	X

(a) (i)   What is the general formula for the alkynes?   **1**

   (ii)   Suggest a name for X.   **1**

(b) The alkynes react with bromine as follows:

$$H-C\equiv C-H + 2\,Br_2 \longrightarrow H-\overset{\overset{\displaystyle Br}{\mid}}{\underset{\underset{\displaystyle Br}{\mid}}{C}}-\overset{\overset{\displaystyle Br}{\mid}}{\underset{\underset{\displaystyle Br}{\mid}}{C}}-H$$

   (i)   Draw the full structural formula of the product when but-1-yne fully reacts with bromine.   **1**

   (ii)   What name is given to this type of reaction?   **1**

Total marks 4

7. Vinegar is made by dissolving ethanoic acid in water. The ethanoic acid is produced when ethanol is oxidised.

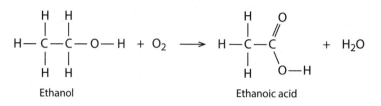

Ethanol   Ethanoic acid

(a) Circle the functional group on ethanoic acid.

1

(b) Vinegar is widely used as flavouring for food. Give another use of vinegar.

1

(c) Ethanol and ethanoic acid react together to form the compound ethyl ethanoate.

(i) What family of compounds does ethyl ethanoate belong to?

1

(ii) The names of some other members of this family are shown in the table below.

Alcohol	Acid	Product
Ethanol	Propanoic acid	Ethyl propanoate
Ethanol	Butanoic acid	Ethyl butanoate
Propanol	Propanoic acid	Propyl propanoate
Butanol	Ethanoic acid	Butyl ethanoate

Name the product when butanol and propanoic acid are reacted.

1

Total marks 4

8. Liquid petroleum gas (LPG) is an alternative fuel to petrol.

Propane is the main gas in LPG. When propane burns it produces energy, carbon dioxide and water.

$$C_3H_8(g) + 5O_2(g) \longrightarrow 3CO_2(g) + 4H_2O(l)$$

(a) What name is given to a reaction where a substance reacts with oxygen to produce heat?

1

(b) LPG is also the fuel found in camping stoves.

A student used a camping stove to boil 2 litres of water. The starting temperature of the water was 23°C and the final temperature was 100°C.

Calculate the energy released in kJ.

3

(c) Propane belongs to the alkane family. The energy released per mole of some alkanes is shown below.

Alkane	Energy kJmol l^{-1} per mole
Propane	2202
Butane	2877
Pentane	3509
Hexane	4163
Heptane	4817
Octane	

(i) Predict the energy released per mole of octane.

1

(ii) An advantage of LPG is that it produces less carbon dioxide per mole than octane, which is the main alkane in petrol.

Suggest a disadvantage of using LPG over petrol.

1

Total marks   6

9. Monster trucks use methanol as a fuel in place of petrol.

(a) To what family of compounds does methanol belong? **1**

(b) Methanol is widely produced by reacting carbon monoxide with hydrogen in the presence of a catalyst.

$$CO(g) + 2H_2(g) \longrightarrow CH_3OH(l)$$

What mass of methanol would be produced by reacting 70 g of carbon monoxide completely with hydrogen? **3**

Total marks 4

10. A student set up the following cell.

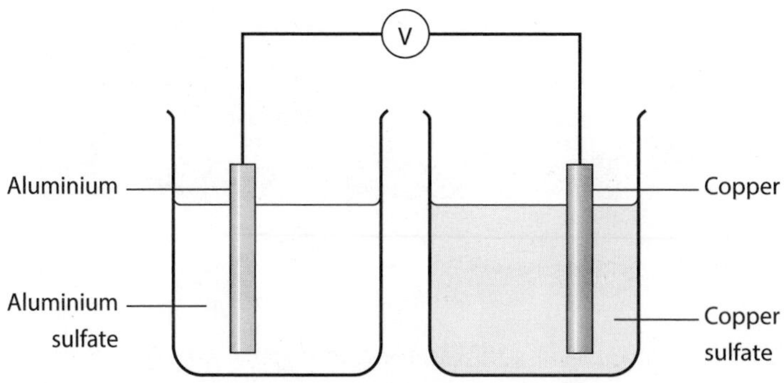

(a) What needs to be added to complete the cell? 1

(b) The following reactions occurred at the electrodes:

$$Al(s) \longrightarrow Al^{3+}(aq) + 3e$$

$$Cu^{2+}(aq) + 2e \longrightarrow Cu(s)$$

  (i) Combine these to form a balanced redox equation. 1

  (ii) Mark the path of electron flow on the diagram using arrows. 1

  (iii) What effect would replacing copper with tin have on the voltage produced? 1

Total marks 4

11. Aluminium is a metal commonly used to build aircraft.

(a) Explain why aluminium is more suitable for making aircraft than iron.

You may wish to use your data booklet to help you.   **1**

(b) Aluminium is the most abundant metal in the Earth's crust where it is commonly found in ores in the form of aluminium hydroxide and aluminium oxide.

The first time aluminium was extracted was in 1825, unlike copper which was extracted in prehistoric times.

Using your knowledge of chemistry, discuss why aluminium, which is more abundant than copper in the Earth's core, was only extracted from ores in recent history.   **3**

Total marks   4

12. Polyisobutene, a synthetic rubber, is a polymer which does not allow air through it. This makes it an important material in cling film, tyre inner tubes and the bladders in footballs.

A section containing three monomers of the polymer is shown below.

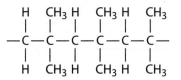

(a) Draw the monomer used to produce polyisobutene.   **1**

(b) Write the systematic name for the monomer above.   **1**

(c) What part of the monomer structure allows polymerisation to take place?   **1**

(d) Butyl rubber is another synthetic rubber based on polyisobutene.

Butyl rubber contains two isobutene monomers joined to another monomer X.

A section of the polymer is shown below. Circle the part of the polymer structure due to monomer X in the structure below.   **1**

Total marks 4

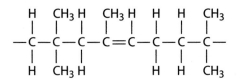

13. Smoke detectors in our homes contain a small amount of the radioisotope Americium 241.

Americium decays to form Neptunium 237.

The first stage in the decay series of Americium is:

(a) Name X.

1

(b) A 24 g sample of Americium took 916 years to decay to 6 g.

Calculate the half life of the sample.

2

Total marks 3

14. Ammonia is an important starting material in the production of nitric acid, HNO_3.

Ammonia can be produced by the reaction between nitrogen and hydrogen.

$$N_2(g) + 3H_2(g) \rightleftharpoons 2NH_3(g)$$

(a) What is meant by the $\rightleftharpoons$ in the above reaction?   **1**

(b) Oxides of nitrogen, NO_x, are needed to make nitric acid.

Oxides of nitrogen are produced by bubbling gas X through a solution of ammonium hydroxide.

These oxides can be produced in the laboratory using the apparatus below.

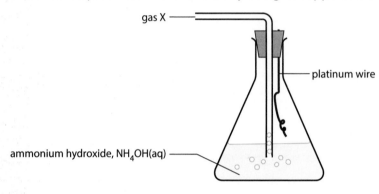

(i)   Name gas X.   **1**

(ii)   The platinum wire is a catalyst and glows red hot as soon as the oxidation takes place.

What word can be used to describe this oxidation reaction?   **1**

(c) The reaction between nitric acid and ammonia produces an important fertiliser.

(i)   Name this fertiliser.   **1**

(ii)   Ammonium phosphate is another fertiliser.

Write the chemical formula for ammonium phosphate.   **1**

Total marks   5

Practice Exam C

N5 Chemistry

Practice Papers for SQA Exams   Exam C

Fill in these boxes:

Full name of centre   Town

Forename(s)   Surname

Try to answer all of the questions in the time allowed.

Total marks – 80

Section 1 – 20 marks

Section 2 – 60 marks

Read all questions carefully before attempting.

You have 2 hours to complete this paper.

Write your answers in the spaces provided, including all of your working.

Scotland's leading educational publishers

SECTION 1

1. Magnesium reacts with hydrochloric acid to form hydrogen gas. The speed of the reaction can be measured by recording the volume of hydrogen gas produced per minute.

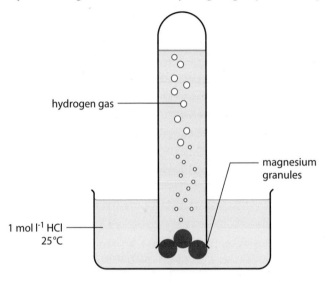

Which experiment would you use to investigate the effect of temperature on the above reaction?

A

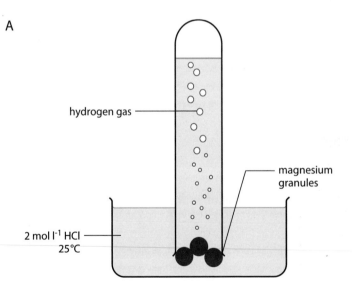

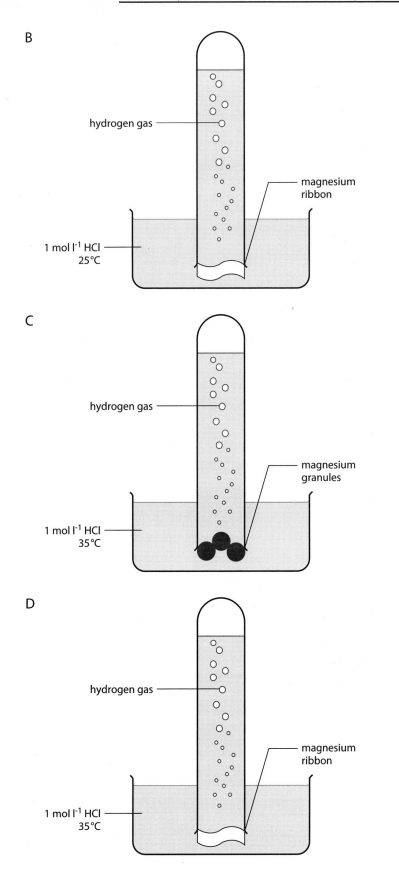

B

hydrogen gas

magnesium ribbon

1 mol l^{-1} HCl
25°C

C

hydrogen gas

magnesium granules

1 mol l^{-1} HCl
35°C

D

hydrogen gas

magnesium ribbon

1 mol l^{-1} HCl
35°C

2. Which set of information describes a proton?

Answer	Mass	Charge	Location
A	1	+1	orbitals/shells
B	1	0	nucleus
C	0	−1	orbitals/shells
D	1	+1	nucleus

3. $^{35}_{17}Cl$ and $^{37}_{17}Cl$ are

A isomers

B isotopes

C ions

D homologous series.

4. Which of the following elements is in the same period as Lithium?

You may wish to use your data booklet to help you.

A Carbon

B Potassium

C Helium

D Magnesium

5. An unknown substance conducts electricity as a solid and as a liquid and is a liquid at room temperature.

The substance could be

A Bromine

B Water

C Magnesium

D Mercury

6. The following apparatus was set up.

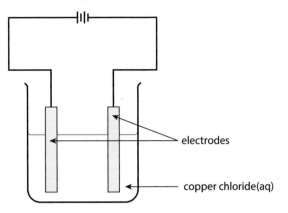

electrodes

copper chloride(aq)

Which set of results matches the above electrolysis?

Answer	Positive	Negative
A	Solid copper	Chorine gas
B	Hydrogen gas	Chlorine gas
C	Chlorine gas	Solid copper
D	Hydrogen gas	Solid copper

7. Hydroxide ions are released when solid barium hydroxide is added to water.

What would be the pH of the resultant solution?

A 6

B 9

C 7

D 6.5

8. 25 cm³ of $Ca(OH)_2$ neutralised 20 cm³ of 0.1 mol l⁻¹ solution of hydrochloric acid, HCl.

What was the concentration of the calcium hydroxide, $Ca(OH)_2(aq)$?

A 0.1 mol l⁻¹

B 0.04 mol l⁻¹

C 0.16 mol l⁻¹

D 0.06 mol l⁻¹

9. The hydrocarbon below belongs to the cycloalkanes.

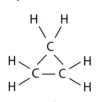

What is the general formula of the cycloalkanes?

A C_nH_n

B C_nH_{2n-2}

C C_nH_{2n}

D C_nH_{2n+2}

10. Which of the following hydrocarbons could be described as saturated?

A C_2H_2

B C_2H_4

C C_2H_6

D C_3H_6

11. Which of the following compounds is a solid at 0°C?

You may wish to use your data booklet to help you.

A Ethanol

B Ethanoic acid

C Propan-1-ol

D Propanoic acid

12. Which of the following compounds is a carboxylic acid?

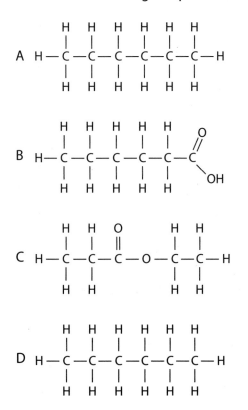

13. Which of the following shows an ester link?

A

$$\underset{\displaystyle }{-\overset{\displaystyle O}{\overset{\displaystyle \|}{C}}-O}$$

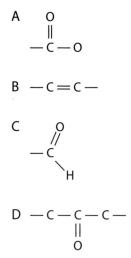

B $-C=C-$

C

$$-\overset{\displaystyle O}{\overset{\displaystyle /\!/}{C}}\underset{\displaystyle \diagdown H}{}$$

D $-C-C-C-$
         ||
         O

Questions **14** and **15** refer to the experiment below.

A student measured the heat energy released when ethanol is burned using the apparatus below.

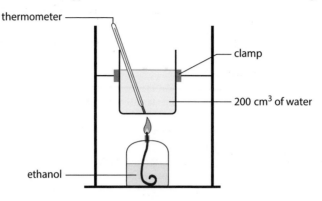

14. The energy released was calculated to be 8.36 kJ.

The initial water temperature was 21°C. What was the final temperature of the water?

A 30°C

B 31°C

C 40°C

D 41°C

15. Which term best describes the burning of ethanol?

A endothermic

B exothermic

C reduction

D redox

16. Which of the following natural compounds is a polymer?

A Amino acid

B Glucose

C Fat

D Starch

17. The ion electron equations for the redox reaction between zinc and silver ions are shown below.

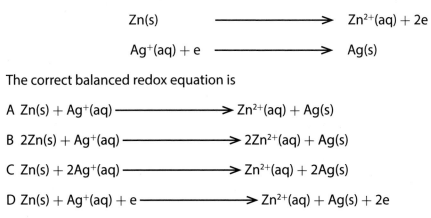

The correct balanced redox equation is

A $Zn(s) + Ag^+(aq) \longrightarrow Zn^{2+}(aq) + Ag(s)$

B $2Zn(s) + Ag^+(aq) \longrightarrow 2Zn^{2+}(aq) + Ag(s)$

C $Zn(s) + 2Ag^+(aq) \longrightarrow Zn^{2+}(aq) + 2Ag(s)$

D $Zn(s) + Ag^+(aq) + e \longrightarrow Zn^{2+}(aq) + Ag(s) + 2e$

18. Which metal will not react with sulphuric acid?

A Silver

B Magnesium

C Aluminium

D Zinc

19. Which of the following diagrams represents metallic bonding?

A

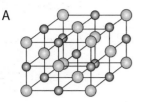

B

C

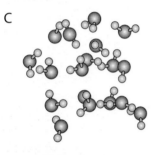

D

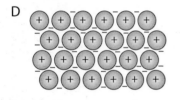

20. Which statement correctly describes what happens during Beta decay.

A An electron is fired out of the nucleus.

B Two protons and two neutrons are fired out of the nucleus.

C A neutron is fired out of the nucleus.

D An electromagnetic wave is released from the nucleus.

N5 Chemistry

Practice Papers for SQA Exams

Exam C

Fill in these boxes:

Full name of centre

Town

Forename(s)

Surname

Section 2 – 60 marks

Attempt all questions.

Scotland's leading educational publishers

MARKS
Do not write in this margin

SECTION 2

1. Zinc reacts with hydrochloric acid to produce hydrogen gas.

    The table below shows the volume of hydrogen gas collected over time for the above reaction.

Time (seconds)	Volume of hydrogen (cm³)
0	0
20	8
40	15
60	21
80	26
100	30
120	34
140	37
160	39
180	40
200	40

    (a) (i) Plot a line graph of the results of the reaction.   3

(ii) Calculate the average rate of reaction between 10 seconds and 40 seconds.

2

(b) This reaction can be increased by the addition of the catalyst copper.

(i) The graph below represents the volume of hydrogen gas evolved over time for the reaction between zinc and acid.

Draw the curve you would expect if the same experiment was repeated with the addition of copper.

1

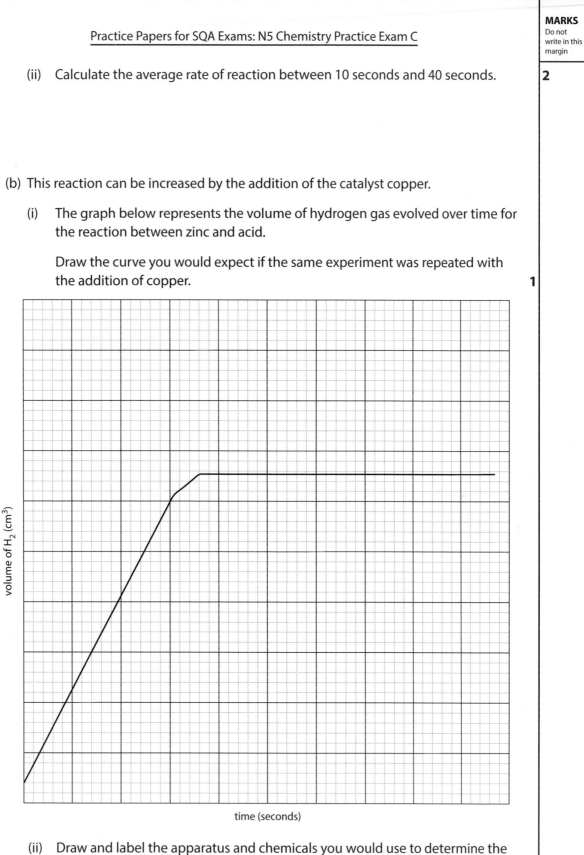

volume of H_2 (cm^3)

time (seconds)

(ii) Draw and label the apparatus and chemicals you would use to determine the volume of hydrogen gas given off when zinc and hydrochloric acid react in the presence of copper.

1

Total marks 7

2. Fuels made from plants are called biofuels.

Ethanol is a biofuel formed from the fermentation of carbohydrates.

The combustion of ethanol is shown below.

$$C_2H_5OH(l) + O_2(g) \longrightarrow CO_2(g) + H_2O(l)$$

(a) (i) Balance the above equation.

1

    (ii) Calculate the mass of oxygen required to burn 9.2 g of ethanol.

3

(b) Methane (biogas) is formed from rotting plant matter.

    (i) Draw the outer electrons in a molecule of methane, CH_4.

1

    (ii) What name is given to the shape a molecule of methane takes?

1

Total marks 6

3. Carbon forms many different compounds. Two such compounds are silicon carbide (SiC) and carbon dioxide.

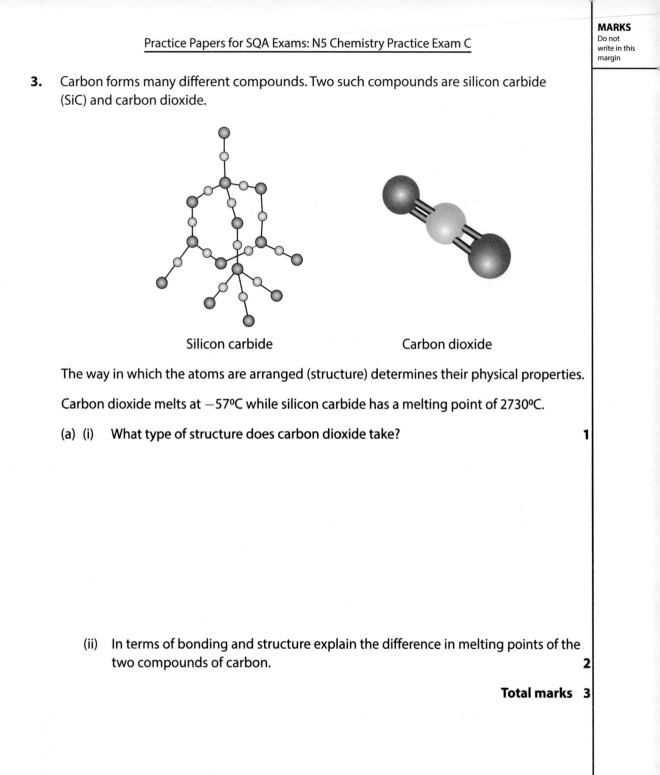

Silicon carbide   Carbon dioxide

The way in which the atoms are arranged (structure) determines their physical properties.

Carbon dioxide melts at $-57^{\circ}C$ while silicon carbide has a melting point of $2730^{\circ}C$.

(a) (i)   What type of structure does carbon dioxide take?   **1**

   (ii) In terms of bonding and structure explain the difference in melting points of the two compounds of carbon.   **2**

Total marks   3

4. Calcium forms many useful products.

One such compound is calcium phosphate which is the main constituent of your skeleton.

(a) Write the formula for calcium phosphate.

1

(b) When calcium reacts it forms the ion Ca^{2+}.

    (i)   In terms of electrons describe the changes in a calcium atom when it reacts to form a calcium ion.

1

    (ii) Explain why calcium forms Ca^{2+} ions and not Ca^{3+} ions.

1

(c) Calcium chloride is another compound of calcium and forms the following structure when solid.

What type of structure is shown below?

1

Total marks 4

calcium (II) chloride

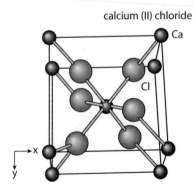

5. The hydrogen halides when dissolved in water form a group of strong acids.

When the hydrogen halides dissolve in water the bond between the hydrogen and the halide is broken and a hydrogen ion is released.

$$HCl(g) \longrightarrow H^+(aq) + Cl^-(aq)$$

The energy required to break the bond between the hydrogen and the halide is called its bond enthalpy.

Hydrogen halide	GFM	Bond enthalpy (kJ mol I^{-1})
HF	20	+569
HCl	36·5	+428
HBr	81	+362
HI	128	

(a) (i) Write a statement linking the gfm of the halide to its bond enthalpy.

You may wish to use your data booklet.   1

(ii) Predict the bond enthalpy of hydrogen iodide (HI).   1

(b) Hydrochloric acid reacts with the alkali calcium hydroxide. The reaction is given.

$$2H^+Cl^-(aq) + Ca^{2+}(OH^-)_2(aq) \longrightarrow Ca^{2+}Cl^-_2(aq) + 2H_2O(l)$$

(i) Circle the salt formed in the above reaction.   1

(ii) Rewrite the above reaction omitting all spectator ions.   1

Total marks 4

6. Ethylchloride is a member of a group of compounds named the chloroalkanes and can be produced by reacting ethene with hydrogen chloride.

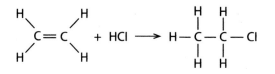

Ethylchloride is used in dentistry to detect dead teeth. A small amount of ethylchloride is sprayed onto a tooth. If the tooth is still alive the patient will feel a chilling effect due to the low boiling point of ethylchloride.

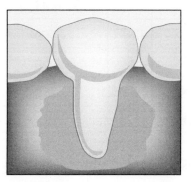

The following table shows the boiling points of some chloroalkanes.

Systematic name	Full structural formula	Boiling point (°C)
1-chloroethane		12
2-chloropropane		36
2-chlorobutane		70
3-chloropentane		96

(a) (i) Draw the full structural formula of the alkene that could be reacted with hydrogen chloride to make 3-chloropentane.

1

(ii) Name the type of chemical reaction which takes place when alkenes react with hydrogen chloride.

1

(b) Propene reacts with hydrogen in a similar way.

(i) Name the product of the reaction between propene and hydrogen.

1

(ii) Cyclopropane and propene are isomers of each other.

State what is meant by the term isomer.

1

(iii) When bromine water is added to each hydrocarbon the following colour changes take place.

Colour change	Hydrocarbon
No change	
Yellow to clear	

Complete the table to show which hydrocarbon, cyclopropane and propene, give which result when added to bromine water.

1

Total marks 5

7. Alcohols are often found in hand gels. Alcohol based hand sanitisers are more effective at killing bacteria than soaps and do not dry out skin as much.

The main ingredient in hand gels is

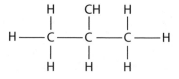

(a) (i) Name the alcohol used in hand gels.

1

(ii) What name is given to the functional group present in all alcohols?

1

(b) The alcohol in (a) was formed from an alkene.

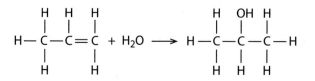

Two alcohols were formed, one of which is shown.

Draw the full structural formula of the other alcohol.

1

(c) Alcohols can be easily converted to carboxylic acids.

What family of compounds is formed when alcohols and carboxylic acids react?

1

Total marks 4

8. Iron is extracted from iron ore industrially in a blast furnace.

In a blast furnace iron oxide is reacted with carbon dioxide to produce iron metal and carbon dioxide.

$$Fe_2O_3(s) + 3CO(g) \longrightarrow 2Fe(s) + 3CO_2(g)$$

(a) What is the charge on the iron ion in the iron oxide?　　　　　　　　　**1**

(b) Write an ion electron equation for the reduction of iron in a blast furnace.　　**1**

(c) Iron is used to make large structures such as bridges and buildings.

　　Explain how iron structures can be damaged by acid rain.　　　　　**1**

Total marks　3

9. Pheromones are special natural chemicals that trigger a response when released.

Female Asian elephants release the following molecule in their urine to signal that they are ready to mate.

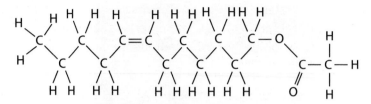

Using your knowledge of chemistry, discuss the chemical and physical properties of this pheromone.

3

Total marks   3

10. Read the following passage carefully and answer the questions which follow.

Rechargeable batteries

An entirely new type of material developed at Rensselaer Polytechnic Institute could enable the next generation of high-power rechargeable lithium-ion (Li-ion) batteries for electric automobiles, as well as batteries for laptop computers, mobile phones and other portable devices.

The positive electrode (anode) in a Li-ion battery physically grows and shrinks as the battery charges or discharges, when in use. When charging the addition of Li-ions increases the volume of the electrode, while discharging has the opposite effect. These volume changes result in a build-up of stress in the anode. Too great a stress that builds up too quickly, as in the case of a battery charging or discharging at high speeds, can cause the battery to fail prematurely. This is why most batteries in today's portable electronic devices like cell phones and laptops charge very slowly – the slow charge rate is intentional and designed to protect the battery from stress-induced damage.

The Rensselaer team's nanoscoop positive electrode, however, was engineered to withstand this build-up of stress. Made from a carbon base topped with a thin layer of aluminum (Al) and a 'scoop' of silicon (Si), the structures are flexible and able to quickly accept and discharge Li-ions at extremely fast rates without sustaining significant damage.

The segmented structure of the nanoscoop allows the strain to be gradually transferred from the C base to the Al layer, and finally to the Si scoop. This natural strain gradation provides for a less abrupt transition in stress across the material interfaces, leading to improved structural integrity of the electrode.

This passage was adapted from the article 'Nanoscoops could spark new generation of electric automobile batteries' by Rensselaer Polytechnic Institute, published on the science daily.com, January 2011.

(a) Name **one** of the elements used to make the 'nanoscoop'.　　　　　　　**1**

(b) Oxidation and reduction reactions take place at the positive electrode (anode) depending on whether you are charging your cell or it is discharging and powering an appliance.

　　Describe the difference between an oxidation and reduction reaction.　　**1**

(c) Why is the new electrode not made of lithium metal?　　　　　　　**1**

Total marks　3

11. Polyesters are an important group of polymers.

The reaction below shows the formation of a polyester.

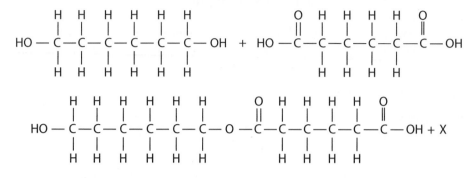

(a) Name molecule X.

1

(b) What type of polymerisation is taking place?

1

(c) Draw part of a polymer chain formed from the reaction between one each of the following monomers.

2

Total marks 4

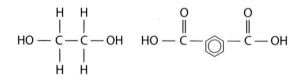

MARKS Do not write in this margin

12. Carbon has three isotopes. Carbon 12 and carbon 13 are stable.

The third isotope is carbon 14, which is unstable.

The decay of carbon 14 is shown below.

$$^{14}_{6}C \longrightarrow {}^{14}_{7}N + X$$

(a) Name particle X. **1**

(b) State **one** use of the carbon 14 isotope. **1**

(c) Carbon 14 has a half life of 5730 years. How long would it take for a 20 g sample to decay to 2.5g? **1**

(d) If a sample of carbon 14 was heated, what effect would this have on its half life? **1**

Total marks 4

13. Ammonia is an important starter material for the production of fertilisers.

The diagram below shows the stages in the production of ammonia.

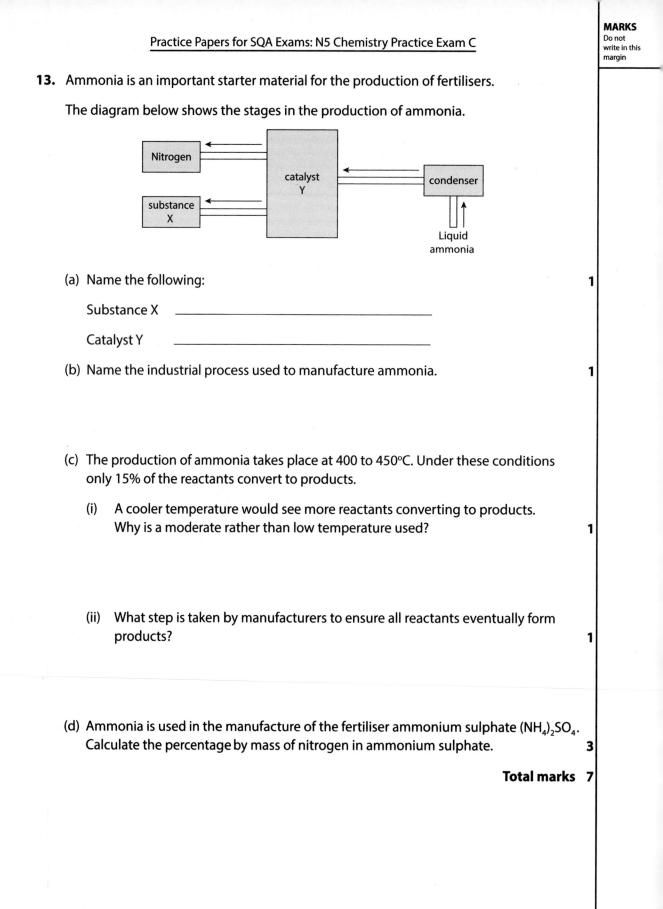

(a) Name the following: 1

Substance X _____

Catalyst Y _____

(b) Name the industrial process used to manufacture ammonia. 1

(c) The production of ammonia takes place at 400 to 450°C. Under these conditions only 15% of the reactants convert to products.

(i) A cooler temperature would see more reactants converting to products. Why is a moderate rather than low temperature used? 1

(ii) What step is taken by manufacturers to ensure all reactants eventually form products? 1

(d) Ammonia is used in the manufacture of the fertiliser ammonium sulphate $(NH_4)_2SO_4$. Calculate the percentage by mass of nitrogen in ammonium sulphate. 3

Total marks 7

MARKS
Do not
write in this
margin

14. A student was given three unlabelled bottles.

Each bottle contained one of the oxides below.

Potassium oxide   Copper oxide   Silver oxide

Using your knowledge of chemistry, describe how the pupil could determine which bottle contained which oxide. **3**

Total marks   3

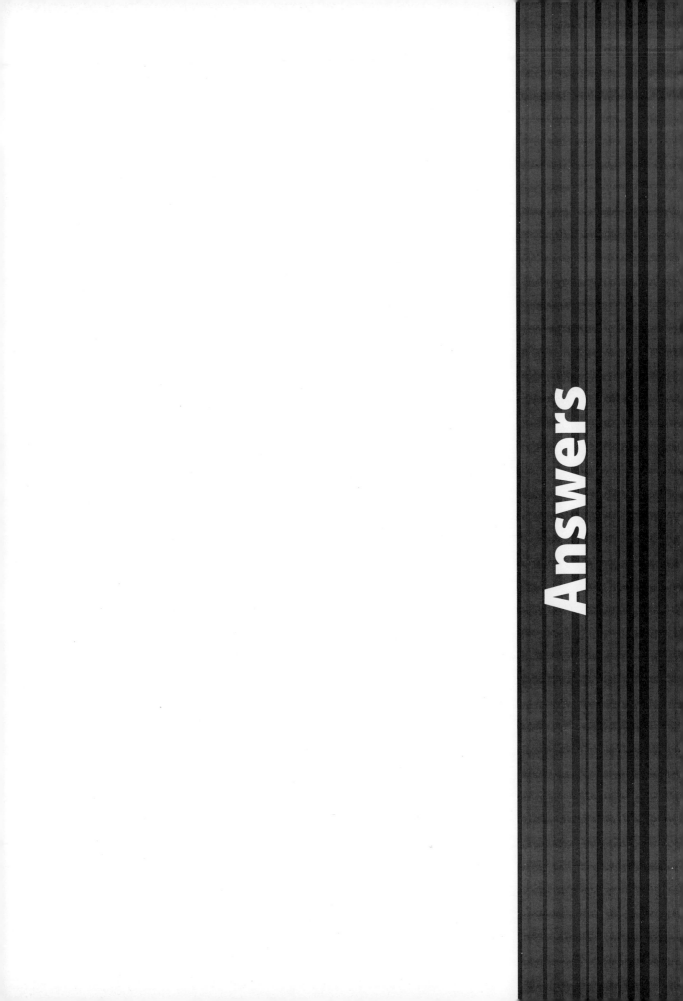

Answers

Answers to Practice Exams

Practice Exam A Worked Answers

Section 1

The following marking scheme is a guide only and is the interpretation of the authors of these papers.

1. B As the particle size increases (i.e. from powder to lumps) the reaction slows down. The mass/concentration of a reactant will only affect the mass/volume of products made and not the speed of reaction.

2. B Ionic bonds are the electrostatic attraction between positive metal ions and negative non metal ions. B is the only answer that contains metals and non metals. **Make sure you use your data booklet to check this type of question.**

3. C Metals conduct in all states. Ionic substances only conduct as liquids or in solution, while covalent substances do not conduct.

4. C Group 8 elements (noble gases) are stable and have 8 outer electrons.

5. D $NaOH + HCl \longrightarrow NaCl + H_2O$

moles of NaOH = moles of HCl

moles of NaOH = $C \times V = 1 \times 0.02 = 0.02$ moles

concentration of HCl $= \dfrac{n}{V} = \dfrac{0.02}{0.04} = 0.5$ mol l^{-1}

6. A Atoms of the same element have the same atomic number. Neutrons (isotopes) and electrons (ions) can change.

7. B Longest straight chain has 4 carbons – butane. **Two** methyl branches coming off this chain occur on the 2, 3 carbon – 2, 3 **di** methyl.

8. A A combustion reaction is a chemical reaction between a substance and oxygen, producing energy?

9. A C=C bond breaks and bromine adds on.

10. C

11. D

12. A Metal carbonates react with acids to give salt, water and carbon dioxide. Carbon dioxide is the gas that turns limewater cloudy.

13. B The larger the difference between the metals in the electrochemical series the bigger the voltage.

14. D Metals more reactive than zinc need to be extracted by electrolysis.

15. B A reducing agent helps extract the metal.

16. C Only metals higher in the electrochemical series will react with solutions containing less reactive metals.

17. C

18. B

19. C

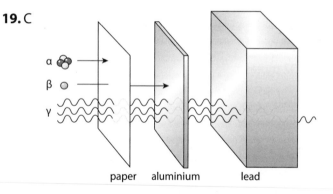

20. C (i)   Metal carbonates and metals react with acids to form carbon dioxide and hydrogen gas.
   (ii)   Copper compounds burn with a blue-green colour (see data booklet).
   (iii) A is not an option as copper does not react with acids.

Section 2

1. (a) Make sure you have:

- Labels and units for each axis (copy the headings from the table). **1**

- Correct scales (if you can, go up in 1, 2, 5, 10, 50 or 100s). **1**

- Correct points and a line through those points. **1**

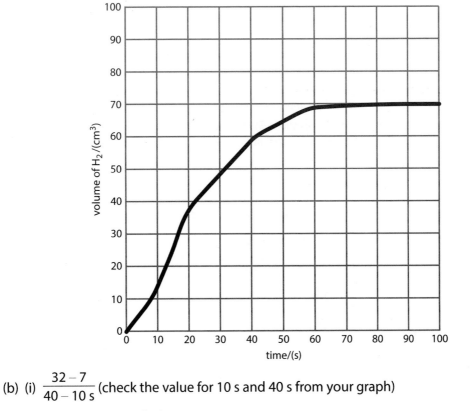

(b) (i) $\dfrac{32-7}{40-10 \text{ s}}$ (check the value for 10 s and 40 s from your graph) **1**

$= 0.83$ or $0.8 \text{ cm}^3\text{s}^{-1}$ **1**

> **HINT** *Make sure you read off your graph or table at the correct times, in this case 10 and 40 seconds. If your graph is drawn slightly differently you may get a different answer.*

(ii) Any value more than that given in b (i) as a more concentrated acid would result in a faster reaction. **1**

2. (a) $(Cu^+)_2 (S^{2-})$ **1**

   (b) ^{63}Cu **1**

   (c) (i) Ion   **1**

       (ii) Protons = Atomic number = 29
           Neutrons = Mass number − Atomic number = 63 − 29 = 34   **1**

> **HINT**   *Both must be correct for 1 mark.*

         Since Cu^{2+} has two more protons than electrons, the number of electrons is 27.   **1**

3.

> **HINT**   *The following answer is the authors' interpretation of this open question.*
> *The list below gives some suggestions and to obtain full marks not all points described need to be raised. For full marks candidates must show a good understanding of the chemistry.*

- Description of metallic bonding
- Description of covalent bonding, both molecular and network
- Discussion of properties of metallic elements
- Discussion of properties of covalent elements
- Explanation of why metallic elements conduct
- Explanation of why covalent elements do not conduct
- Discussion of α's structure
- Explanation of graphite's properties   **3, 2 or 1**

4. (a) It donates or gives hydrogen ions to the sea water, it increases the hydrogen ion content of the sea water.   **1**

   (b) Photosynthetic algae require CO_2 to photosynthesise.   **1**

   (c) Alkanes burn to give off carbon dioxide, which is an acid gas.   **1**

5. (a) The sodium and chloride symbols must be circled, i.e. $(Na^+)_2$ CO^{2-}_3, H^+ (Cl^-) or (Na^+Cl^-) **1**

> **HINT**   *Be careful when drawing the circles, making sure you only put the circles around the correct ions and not others next to it.*

   (b) (i) $n = C \times V = 0.1 \times 0.25$ **1**

              $= 0.025$ moles   **1**

(ii) Mass $= n \times gfm = 0.025 \times 106$ **1**

     $= 2.65$ **1**

$$Na_2CO_3 = 2 \times Na \;=\; 2 \times 23 \;=\quad 46$$
$$ 1 \times C \quad\; 1 \times 12 \qquad 12$$
$$ 3 \times O \quad\; 3 \times 16 \qquad \underline{48}$$
$$ \text{Total } 106$$

(c) Student A   **1**

The overall volume of the solute and the solvent should be 250 cm³.

Student B had 250 cm³ of water plus the volume of sodium carbonate, which is more than 250 cm³.   **1**

6. (a) $E = cm\Delta t$ **1**

    $= 4.18 \times 0.1 \times 8$ **1**

    $= 3.34 \text{ kJ}$ **1**

(b) Heat shield to prevent heat lost to surroundings or other acceptable answer   **1**

(c) (i) CnH_{2n+2} **1**

    (ii) Any molecule with 1 or 2 less carbons in the main chain, added on as branches. i.e.   **1**

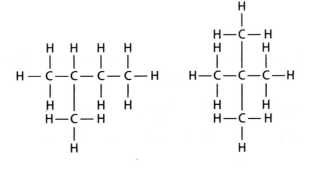

7. (a) (i)

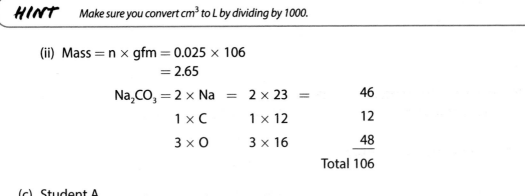

                    1

(ii) A family of compounds with the same general formula and similar chemical properties.   **1**

(b) 100 to 110   **1**

(c) (i) H_2 or hydrogen   1

(ii) The functional group, C=O, must be at the end of the molecule for it to be an aldehyde. 1

8. (a) (i) moles of CH_3COOH = moles of H_2O

moles of $CH_3COOH = \dfrac{1.5}{60}$ $\dfrac{\text{(mass)}}{\text{(gfm)}} = 0.025$ moles   1

moles of H_2O $= 0.025$ moles   1

mass of H_2O $= n \times gfm = 0.025 \times 18 = 0.45$ g   1

0.45g on its own would gain 3 marks, but we would always advise you to lay out your calculation, showing all working clearly.

(ii) Potassium ethanoate   1

(b) Preservative or other acceptable answer.   1

9. (a) $(NH_4)_2SO_4(s) + 2\,NaOH(s) \longrightarrow Na_2SO_4(s) + 2NH_3(g) + 2\,H_2O(l)$ 1

(b) blue/purple or black   1

(c) $\dfrac{2N}{(NH_4)_2SO_4} = \dfrac{2 \times 14}{(2 \times 18) + 32 + (16 \times 4)}$ 1

$= \dfrac{28}{132} \times 100$ 1

$= 21\%$ 1

3 marks for 21% only

10. (a) (i) The time for half of the nuclei of a particular isotope to decay.   1

(ii) $20 - 10 \quad = 87.7$ years

$10 - 5 \quad = 87.7$ years

$5 - 2.5 \quad = 87.7$ years

$2.5 - 1.25 = 87.7$ years   1

Total $= 50.8$ years   1

(b) (i) Any one of Alpha particle/helium nucleus/α particle   1

(ii) Long half life   1

11.

> The following answer is the authors' interpretation of this open question.
>
> *HINT* The list below gives some suggestions and to obtain full marks not all points described need to be raised. For full marks candidates must show a good understanding of the chemistry involved.

- Both molecules contain a carboxylic acid group and these can react with alcohols to form esters.
- Both will have a pH of below 7.
- Both will have H^+ ions when dissolved in water.
- Both can form salts when reacted with bases.
- The fatty acid of the fat is mainly an alkane molecule as they contain carbon to carbon single bonds only. Alkane molecules are saturated and therefore generally won't react. They take place in substitution reactions.
- The fatty acid in an oil contains a carbon to carbon double bond; therefore they take place in addition reactions.
- Description of addition reactions.
- A fatty acid in an oil can be converted to a fatty acid such as that found in a fat by reacting the oil molecule with hydrogen.   **3, 2 or 1**

12. (a) (i) Oxidation   **1**

(ii) $O_2(g) + 4H^+(aq) + 2H_2(g) \longrightarrow 4H^+(aq) + 2H_2O(l)$

Or $O_2(g) + 2H_2(g) \longrightarrow 2H_2O(l)$ **1**

(iii)

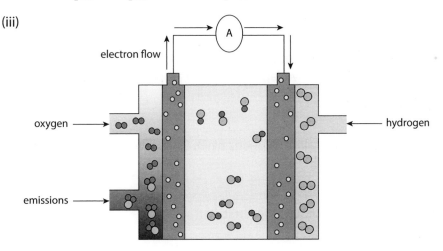

Electron flow must not be on wires and should not go near the solutions.   **1**

13. (a)

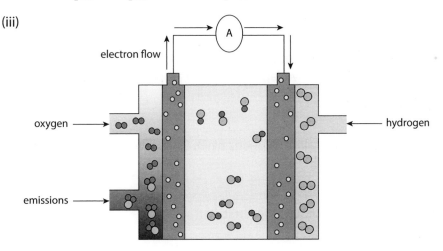

     1

(b) Addition   **1**

(c) (i) OH group   **1**

(ii) Ester group/link   **1**

Practice Exam B Worked Answers

Section 1

The following marking scheme is a guide only and is the interpretation of the authors of these papers.

1. C   Fluorine is in group 7 of the Periodic Table. Group 7 elements are named the halogens.

2. C   Nitrogen gains three electrons to become like neon.

3. D   The -ate ending of sulfate signifies that it contains oxygen as well as sulfur. Ammonium contains nitrogen and hydrogen but since the ammonium compound is a hydride it only contains two elements.

4. B   When in solid form the ions in an ionic compound are held in a 3D lattice so are not free to move. However, when dissolved or melted the lattice breaks allowing the ions to move and conduct electricity.

5. C

6. D   Each carbon atom requires four bonds and each oxygen atom requires two bonds, thus two orbitals from each oxygen overlap with two of carbon's orbitals to form two double bonds.

7. C   Soluble metal oxides form alkaline solutions when they dissolve in water. You can check solubility in your data booklet.

8. B   Solids can be separated from liquids by filtration.

9. D   A is propene, B is but-1-ene, C is 2 methylpropene and D is cyclobutane. Boiling points for organic compounds can be found in your data booklet.

10. D   Isomers have the same chemical formula but different structural formula. 2 methylhexane has the formula C_7H_{16}. Both C and D have this formula but C is 2 methylhexane so is not an isomer.

11. C   Both cycloalkanes and alkenes have the general formula C_nH_{2n}.

12. C Esters are commonly used for solvents, perfumes and flavourings.

13. D The COOH (carboxyl) group signifies a carboxylic acid. Since the example has three carbons it is propanoic acid.

14. C Saturated means a compound that contains only single bonds (an alkane) so must fit into the general formula C_nH_{2n+2}.

15. C Only very unreactive metals such as gold, silver and mercury are found uncombined.

16. B Only metals below hydrogen in the electrochemical series (data booklet, page 10) do not react with acids. Gold can be extracted from its ore by heating so metal X must be copper.

17. C A reducing agent is a species that helps a reduction reaction occur. Extracting iron from its ore is a reduction reaction so carbon monoxide must be the reducing agent.

18. C Answer would be c as remainder are either insoluble or do not contain one of the essential elements for healthy plant growth, (N,P,K).

19. B Alpha radiation gets stopped even by thin sheets of paper so could not be used. A radioisotope with a long half life would be preferable as it has to last for a period of time – if it did not last, production would need to be stopped to replace the isotope.

20. C Ammonia is produced in the Haber process using iron as a catalyst.

Section 2

1. (a) $Al_2(CO_3)_3(s) + 6HCl(aq) \longrightarrow 2AlCl_3(aq) + 3H_2O(l) + 3CO_2(g)$ **1**

   (b) (i) Loss of gas, gas escapes or similar.   **1**

          When a metal carbonate and acid react carbon dioxide gas is formed. Since the reaction vessel is not sealed this gas will escape, meaning the mass will decrease.

        (ii) $\dfrac{51-15}{70-20} = 0.72$ or 0.7 gs^{-1} (check the value for 20 s and 70 s from your graph)   **1**

> **HINT**   *Make sure you read off your graph or table at the correct times, in this case 20 and 70 seconds.*

       (iii) The concentration (of reactants) decreases.

           As any reaction proceeds the concentration of reactants falls. As concentration falls, so does the reaction rate.   **1**

2. (a) (i) Atomic number 87

           Mass number 223   **1**

> **HINT**   *Both must be correct for 1 mark.*

           The atomic number is the number of protons. The mass number is the number of protons plus neutrons.

       (ii) $^{223}_{87}\text{Fr}^+$ **1**

           1 mark for correctly placing atomic and mass numbers.

       (iii) In nuclide notation the mass number always goes above the atomic number to the left of the symbol. Since there are 87 protons and 86 electrons one electron must have been lost, producing a single positive ion. 1 mark for correct charge.   **1**

   (b) Same atomic number but different mass number or same number of protons but different number of neutrons.   **1**

3. (a) Covalent network   **1**

        Boron and nitrogen are both non metals so will bond covalently. The fact that it can absorb other materials suggests a large structure so must be a network.

   (b) 300 grams   **1**

    1 gram absorbs 30 grams of oil so 10 grams will absorb $10 \times 30 = 300$ grams.

4. (a) The first result in a titration is rough/not accurate and is not used in calculations. **1**

(b) (i) NaOH $\quad n = C \times V = 0.1 \times 0.088$

$$= 0.0088 \text{ moles}$$ **1**

2 moles of NaOH requires 1 mole of tartaric acid **1**

0.0088 moles of NaOH goes to 4.4×10^{-3} moles of tartaric acid (**in 25 cm^3**) **1**

HINT   *Make sure you convert cm^3 to L by dividing by 1000.*

(ii) $H_2C_4H_4O_6$ $6 \times H$ 6×1 6

$\quad\quad\quad\quad = 4 \times C = 4 \times 12 =$ 48

$\quad\quad\quad\quad 6 \times O \quad 6 \times 16$ $\underline{96}$

                     Total 150 **1**

Mass $= n \times gfm = 4.4 \times 10^{-3} \times 150$

$\quad\quad\quad = 0.66 \text{ g}$ **1**

5. (a) (i) Acidic salts are made from strong acids and weak alkalis. **1**

(ii) 7 or neutral **1**

Strong acids react with strong alkalis to give neutral salts.

(b)

HINT   *The following answer is the authors' interpretation of this open question.*
You can either describe some of the following points in detail or give a broad answer
mentioning a number of ways in which the pH of an acid can be increased. The list below
gives some suggestions and to obtain full marks not all points described need to be raised.
For full marks candidates must show a good understanding of the chemistry involved.

General chemistry

- Neutral substances have a pH of 7.

- Neutral substances have the same number of H^+ and OH^-.

- An acid has more H^+ ions than water or more H^+ than OH^- ions.

Water

- Dilution means the addition of water.

- Diluting an acid lowers the concentration of H^+ ions.

- Diluting an acid increases the pH until it reaches 7.

- Water dissociates as follows $H_2O \rightleftharpoons H^+ + OH^-$.

Metal oxides and metal carbonates

- In each reaction salt and water are formed.

- Carbonates also produce carbon dioxide.

- Equations omitting the spectator ions to show neutralisation reaction.   **3, 2 or 1**

6. (a) (i) C_nH_{2n-2} **1**

   (ii) Pent-1-yne   **1**

   Five carbons so must have 'pent' prefix. The triple bond is between the first
   two carbons so 1-yne.

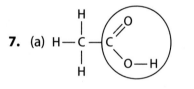

   (b) (i)

   The triple bond breaks leaving four spaces for bromine to add to.   **1**

   (ii) Addition   **1**

   Any reaction that involves double or triple bonds breaking is an addition reaction.

7. (a)   **1**

   (b) Preservative or cleaning product

   (c) (i) Esters   **1**

   Carboxylic acids and alcohols react to give esters.

   (ii) Butyl propanoate   **1**

   The ending of the alcohol used is changed from anol to yl so butyl.

   The ending of the acid used is changed from -oic acid to -oate so propanoate.

8. (a) Combustion   1

(b) $E = cm\Delta t$ 1

$\quad = 4.18 \times 2 \times 77$ 1

$\quad = 743.32 \text{ kJ}$ 1

(c) (i) $5449 - 5471$ 1

The biggest rise is 654 and the smallest is 632 so your answer should show a rise between these two values.

(ii) LPG produces less energy than petrol.   1

9. (a) The alcohols or alkanols.   1

(b) 1 mole of CO = 1 mole of CH_3OH

moles of CO = mass/gfm = 70/28 = 2.5 moles   1

moles of CH_3OH = 2.5 moles   1

mass of CH_3OH = moles $\times$ gfm = 2.5 $\times$ 32 = 80 g   1

80 g on its own would gain 3 marks, but we would always advise you to lay out your calculation, showing all working clearly.

10. (a) Salt bridge or ion bridge or description.   1

(b) (i) $2Al + 3Cu^{2+} \longrightarrow 2Al^{3+} + 3Cu$

When balancing a redox equation the number of electrons in the oxidation and reduction equations should be balanced. In this case the oxidation reaction needs to be multiplied by 2.

$\quad 2Al \longrightarrow 2Al^{3+} + 6e$

And the reduction reaction needs to be multiplied by 3.

$\quad 3Cu^{2+} + 6e \longrightarrow 3Cu$

The equations can then be combined after cancelling out the electrons.   1

(ii)   1

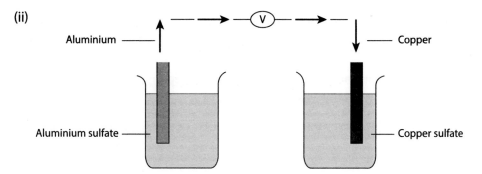

The electrons flow from the metal higher in the electrochemical series (aluminium) to the lower metal (copper). The electrochemical series can be found in your data booklet. The electrons flow only through the wires so care should be taken to make sure your arrows are only on or near to the wires and not in the solutions or salt bridge.

(iii) It would lower the voltage. **1**

The bigger the difference between the metals in the electrochemical series, the bigger the voltage produced.

11. (a) Aluminium is less dense than iron. **1**

(b)

> *HINT* The following answer is the authors' interpretation of this open question. The list below gives some suggestions and to obtain full marks not all points described need to be raised. For full marks candidates must show a good understanding of the chemistry.

- Aluminium is a reactive metal which forms strong attraction between the positive aluminium ions and negative non metal ions.

- A description of some of the reactions of aluminium.

- To extract aluminium the bonds between the positive ions and negative ions must be broken.

- Extraction of a metal is a reduction reaction.

- Aluminium is extracted by electrolysis.

- Electrolysis is the separation of an ionic compound using electricity.

- Electricity only available since 1800s.

- You could describe what happens during electrolysis.

- When an ionic substance is melted or dissolved the ionic acid breaks down, allowing the ions to move. Therefore heat is required.

- The reduction of aluminium ions $Al^{3+} + 3e \longrightarrow Al$. **3, 2 or 1**

12. (a)

$$H \quad CH_3$$
$$| \qquad |$$
$$C = C$$
$$| \qquad |$$
$$H \quad CH_3$$

1

(b) 2 methyl propene or 2 methyl prop-1-ene **1**

As it has 3 carbons in its longest chain and methyl group on the 2nd carbon. The double bond in propene is always between carbons 1 and 2.

But as it contains 4 carbons, 2 ene as double bond is between second and third carbons.

(c) The double bond. **1**

(d)

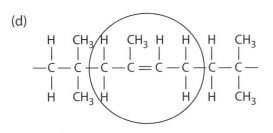

1

13. (a) Any Alpha particle, helium nucleus or symbols

1

The atomic number has decreased by 2 and the mass number has decreased by 4 alpha decay.

(b) $24 - 12 = 1$ half life

$12 - 6 = 2$ half lives

1

$\dfrac{916}{2} = 458$ years

1

14. (a) Reversible reaction

1

(b) (i) Oxygen

1

(ii) Exothermic

1

As the wire is glowing red hot heat must be released, meaning the reaction is exothermic.

(c) (i) Ammonium nitrate

1

If you are not asked for a formula, do not write a formula. Write the name as you may write the wrong formula and lose the mark.

(ii) $(NH_4)_3(PO_4)$

1

Ammonium (NH_4) has a single positive charge thus a valency of 1.

Phosphate has a three negative charge thus a valency of 3.

Practice Exam C Worked Answers

Section 1

The following marking scheme is a guide only and is the interpretation of the authors of these papers.

1. C   All other variables should remain constant except for temperature.

2. D

3. B

4. A   Look at the Periodic Table in the data booklet. Elements in the same row are in the same period.

5. D   Metals are the only substance which conduct in all states and mercury is the only liquid metal.

6. C   Copper (metal) ions are positive and so are attracted to the negative electrode. Chloride ions (non metals) are negative and so are attracted to the positive electrode.

7. B   Alkali solutions have excess hydroxide ions ($Ba(OH)_2$) and therefore pH is greater than 7.

8. B $Ca(OH)_2 + 2HCl \longrightarrow CaCl_2 + 2H_2O$

moles of HCl $= C \times V = 0.1 \times 20 \times 10^{-3}$ (always convert cm³ to L)

$= 0.002$ moles

moles of $Ca(OH)_2 = \dfrac{0.002}{2} = 0.001$ moles

concentration of $Ca(OH)_2 = \dfrac{n}{V} = \dfrac{0.001}{25} \times 10^{-3} = 0.04$ mol l^{-1}

9. C

10. C   Alkanes are saturated as they contain single bonds, general formula of alkanes is C_nH_{2n+2}.

11. B   Look up melting points in the data booklet.

12. B

13. A

14. B $\quad E = cm\Delta t, \Delta t = \dfrac{E}{cm}, \Delta t = \dfrac{8.36}{4.18} \times 0.2$ (convert cm^3 to Kg) $= 10°C$ therefore $31°C$

15. B $\quad$ Energy is given off during combustion reactions – exothermic reaction.

16. D

17. C $\quad$ Multiply second equation by 2 to equal electrons lost in equation one, then add reaction together.

18. A $\quad$ Copper and any metal below copper in the reactivity series will not react with acids.

19. D $\quad$ Diagram represents positive metal's ions in a sea of electrons.

20. A

Section 2

1. (a) (i) Make sure you have:

  • ̣ Labels and units for each axis (copy the headings from the table).   **1**

  • Correct scales (if you can, go up in 1, 2, 5, 10, 50 or 100s).   **1**

  • Correct points and a line through those points.   **1**

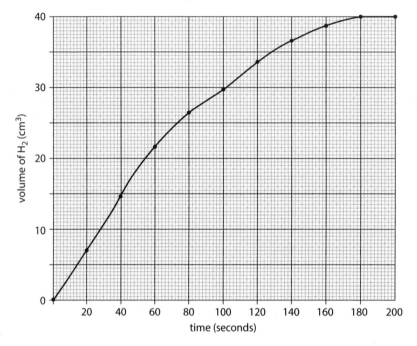

(ii) Reading off the graph:

10 seconds $= 4$ cm^3 40 seconds $= 15$ cm^3

rate of reaction $= \dfrac{15 - 4}{40 - 10}$ cm^3 **1**

Rate of reaction $= 0.366$ or 0.37 cm^3 s^{-1} **1**

> **HINT**   *It is good practice to include units.*

(b) (i) The plot should be

  • steeper

  • level out at the same position.

(Addition of catalyst just speeds up the reaction but does not alter the volume of products.)

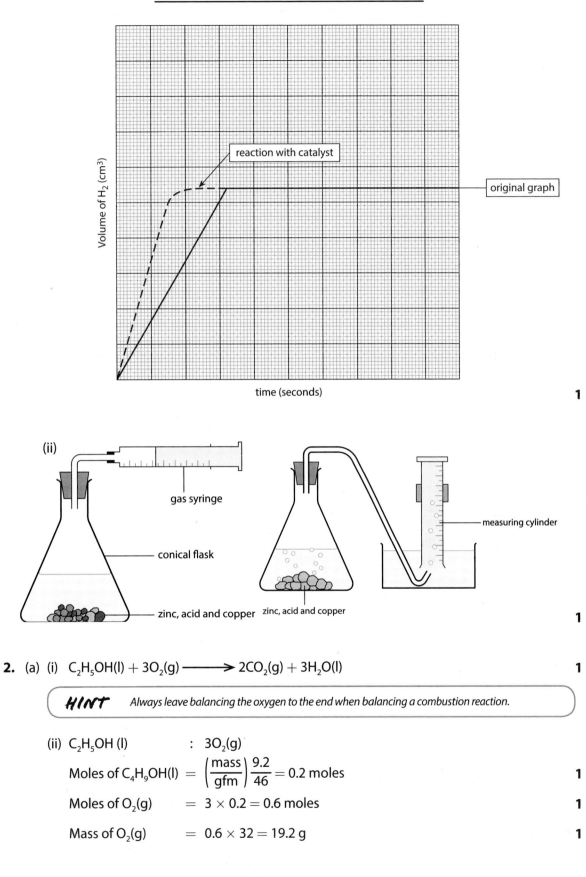

time (seconds)　　　　　　**1**

(ii)

gas syringe

conical flask

zinc, acid and copper　　zinc, acid and copper

measuring cylinder

1

2. (a) (i) $C_2H_5OH(l) + 3O_2(g) \longrightarrow 2CO_2(g) + 3H_2O(l)$ 　　**1**

> **HINT**　　*Always leave balancing the oxygen to the end when balancing a combustion reaction.*

(ii) C_2H_5OH (l)　　　　　:　$3O_2(g)$

Moles of $C_4H_9OH(l) = \left(\dfrac{\text{mass}}{\text{gfm}}\right) \dfrac{9.2}{46} = 0.2$ moles　　**1**

Moles of $O_2(g) = 3 \times 0.2 = 0.6$ moles　　**1**

Mass of $O_2(g) = 0.6 \times 32 = 19.2$ g　　**1**

(b) (i)

Ensure that the electrons are within the orbital overlap. 1

    (ii) Tetrahedral 1

3. (a) (i) Covalent molecular 1

    (ii) Silicon carbide – covalent network structure, strong covalent bonds in structure. 1

        Carbon dioxide – covalent molecular with weak forces of attraction between molecules. 1

4. (a) $Ca_3(PO_4)_2$

    Ensure numbers are subscript.

    Cannot accept group ion PO_4 without brackets, i.e. $Ca_3PO_{4\,2}$ 1

  (b) (i) Calcium atoms lose two electrons when forming calcium ions.

        Calcium has the electron arrangement 2,8,8,2 and so needs to lose two electrons to become like its nearest noble gas Argon. 1

    (ii) Removal of third electron would be from a full electron shell. 1

  (c) Ionic lattice 1

5. (a) (i) The larger the gfm, the smaller the bond enthalpy or the smaller the gfm, the greater the bond enthalpy. 1

    (ii) 330 to 340 1

  (b) (i) $CaCl_2$ 1

    (ii) $2H^+ + 2OH^- \longrightarrow 2H_2O$

            or

      $H^+ + OH^- \longrightarrow H_2O$ 1

6. (a) (i)

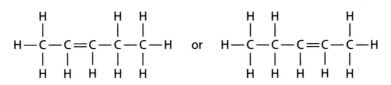

or

1

(ii) Addition (any molecule containing a carbon to carbon double bond will take part in addition reactions). **1**

(b) (i) Propane (alkanes are produced when hydrogen in reacted with alkenes). **1**

(ii) Isomers are molecules with the same molecular formula but different structural formula. **1**

(iii)

Colour change	Hydrocarbon
No change	Cyclopropane
Yellow to clear	Propene

1

7. (a) (i) Propan-2-ol **1**

(ii) Hydroxyl group (OH) **1**

(b)

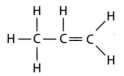

1

(c) Esters **1**

8. (a) Fe^{3+} **1**

(b) $Fe^{3+} + 3e \longrightarrow Fe$ **1**

(c) Iron reacts with acid rain to form iron salts and hydrogen. **1**

9.

> **HINT** The following answer is the authors' interpretation of this open question.
> For full marks candidates must show a good understanding of the chemistry.

• Pheromone is covalently bonded.

• Pheromone is a molecule.

- Pheromone will have low melting point and will not conduct electricity. Explanation of why this is so.

- Pheromone contains ester link.

- Esters have characteristic smell.

- Pheromone has double bond so will undergo addition reactions.   **3, 2 or 1**

10. (a) Any one of: Aluminium, silicon or carbon   **1**

   (b) Oxidation is loss of electrons.

      Reduction is gain of electrons.   **1**

   (c) Lithium is too reactive a metal.   **1**

11. (a) Water/H_2O **1**

   (b) Condensation reaction   **1**

   > **HINT**   *Removal of water is a condensation reaction.*

   (c)

   $$HO - \overset{\overset{\displaystyle H}{|}}{\underset{\underset{\displaystyle H}{|}}{C}} - \overset{\overset{\displaystyle H}{|}}{\underset{\underset{\displaystyle H}{|}}{C}} - O - \overset{\overset{\displaystyle O}{\parallel}}{C} - \overset{}{\underset{}{\bigcirc}} - \overset{\overset{\displaystyle O}{\parallel}}{C} - OH$$

                                                                                              2

12. (a) Beta, β or $_{-1}^{0}e$ **1**

   (b) Carbon dating or description.   **1**

   (c) 20 – 10 1 half life

      10 – 5 2 half lives

      5 – 2.5 3 half lives

      Half life is 5730 years so 3 half lives $3 \times 5730 = 17\ 190$ years.   **1**

   (d) No effect. Half life is not affected by temperature.   **1**

13. (a) X = hydrogen   **1**
      Y = iron

  (b) Haber   **1**

  (c) (i) Reaction is too slow.   **1**

      (ii) Unreacted gases can be recycled.   **1**

  (d) GFM = 132   **1**
     % N = 28 / 132 × 100   **1**
         = 21.2% or 21%   **1**

14.

> *The following answer is the authors' interpretation of this open question.*
> *You can either describe some of the following points in detail (i.e. methods of extraction with reactions, etc.) or give a broad answer mentioning different types of extraction, solubility (pH) and reaction with metals (displacement). The list below gives some suggestions and to obtain full marks not all points described need to be raised. For full marks candidates must show a good understanding of the chemistry.*

Extraction

Silver is extracted from silver oxide by heating alone. Copper oxide requires heating with carbon, while a melt of potassium oxide must be electrolysed. In all reactions the metal is reduced. This answer could be extended by writing equations, writing the reduction reactions, explaining why potassium oxide needs to be melted and what this indicates about the reactivity of potassium, copper and silver.

Solubility, pH (this would be part of a broad answer)

Silver oxide and copper oxide will not dissolve in water but potassium oxide does. The potassium oxide forms a solution of potassium hydroxide, which has a pH less than 7, while the other two would have a pH of 7.

Reactions

You could react each sample with sulfuric acid to form sulfate salts, which are all soluble. The copper sulfate would be blue in colour due to copper ions. Copper would react with silver sulfate to form silver and copper sulfate (a more detailed answer would mention colour changes and half ion electron equations showing the oxidation of the copper and reduction of the silver). Copper sulfate would react with any metal above copper in the reactivity series, again oxidation and reduction reactions can be given.   **3, 2 or 1**